THE FREEMASONS
UNLOCKING THE SECRETS AND MYSTERIES OF THE BROTHERHOOD

by

David Dowson

www.daviddowson.com

daraarts@sky.com

Dedication Page

Acknowledgements
Special thanks to my mother, Beryl, who has always been there for me, and Peter Webber for his advice.

All rights reserved.

No part of this publication may be reproduced or stored in the retrieval system or transmitted, in any form, without the Author's prior permission.

This book may not be reproduced, in whole or in any form, electronic or mechanical, including virtual copying, recording, or by any information storage and retrieval system now known or the hereafter invented without permission of the author.

Edition one
Copyright © David Dowson JUNE 2024
www.daviddowson.com
www.daviddowson.co.uk
daraarts@sky.co.uk

Other books also written by David Dowson include

- Chess for Beginners
- Chess for Beginners Edition 2
- Into the Realm of Chess Calculation
- Nursery Rhymes
- The Path of a Chess Amateur
- CHESS: the BEGINNERS GUIDE eBook

NOVELS

- Declon Five
- Dangers Within
- The Murder of Inspector Hine
- Spooks Scarlett's Enigma
- The Deception Unveiled
- Murder at Buckingham Manor
- Across Bridges SAS on The Line
- Murder at Casanova Hotel
- Uranium 235
- Chapter 2 In The Beginning
- Webs of Blood and Shadows
- Loves Uncharted Path
- Being Mini Lakshmi

Contents

Dedication Page 2
CHAPTER 1 7
CHAPTER 2 16
CHAPTER 3 19
CHAPTER 4 28
CHAPTER 5 38
CHAPTER 6 47
CHAPTER 7 56
CHAPTER 8 65
CHAPTER 9 73
CHAPTER 10 83
CHAPTER 11 93
CHAPTER 12 101
CHAPTER 13 104
CHAPTER 14 107
CHAPTER 15 110
CHAPTER 16 113
CHAPTER 17 116
CHAPTER 18 119
CHAPTER 19 121
CHAPTER 20 127
CHAPTER 21 131
CHAPTER 22 133
CHAPTER 23 135
CHAPTER 24 137
CHAPTER 25 140
CHAPTER 26 142
CHAPTER 23 144
CHAPTER 24 146
CHAPTER 25 148
CHAPTER 26 150

CHAPTER 27 152
About the author 155

CHAPTER 1

Origins of Freemasonry in Ancient Mystery Schools

The ancient mystery schools have long been shrouded in a veil of intrigue and mystique, serving as the foundation for esoteric knowledge that has influenced various spiritual and philosophical traditions throughout history. These revered institutions, dating back to antiquity, were centres of learning and initiation where select individuals were initiated into the mysteries of the universe. Within the hallowed walls of these schools, students delved into the esoteric teachings of astrology, alchemy, sacred geometry, and the mystical arts. The curriculum was designed to expand the consciousness of the initiates, providing them with a deeper understanding of the interconnectedness of the cosmos and their place within it. The mystery schools were not merely academic institutions. Still, they served as spiritual sanctuaries where seekers could commune with the divine and unlock the universe's secrets. It was believed that through rigorous training and initiation rituals, individuals could achieve spiritual enlightenment and transcend the limitations of the material world. As we explore the origins of Freemasonry within the context of these ancient mystery schools, we begin to unravel the intricate tapestry of esoteric knowledge passed down through the ages. By tracing the lineage of Masonic teachings back to these sacred institutions, we gain a deeper appreciation for the rich historical and spiritual legacy that continues to shape the philosophy and practices of Freemasonry today.

The Ancient Mystery Schools: An Overview

Ancient Mystery Schools flourished in civilizations worldwide, serving as centres of esoteric knowledge and spiritual teachings. These schools were revered for their secrecy and commitment to preserving ancient wisdom. Students of the Mystery Schools underwent rigorous training and initiation rituals to gain access to hidden knowledge. The teachings imparted in these schools encompassed a wide range of subjects, including philosophy, metaphysics, astrology, and the mysteries of the cosmos. The Mystery Schools were characterized by their emphasis on the interconnectedness of all things and the pursuit of higher consciousness. They taught that the universe was governed by universal laws and that individuals could attain enlightenment by aligning themselves with these cosmic principles. The symbolism used in the teachings of the Mystery Schools served as a key to unlocking deeper truths and understanding the universe's inner workings. One of the central tenets of the Mystery Schools was the belief in a hidden reality beyond the physical realm. Students were taught that delving into the mysteries of the unseen world could unlock the secrets of existence and achieve spiritual transformation. The teachings of the Mystery Schools were passed down through oral traditions and sacred texts, ensuring the preservation of ancient knowledge for future generations. The legacy of the Mystery Schools lives on in various spiritual traditions, including Freemasonry. The influence of these ancient institutions can be seen in Freemasonry's symbolism, rituals, and philosophical teachings. By delving into the history of the Ancient Mystery Schools, we gain insight into the origins of Freemasonry and the enduring quest for spiritual enlightenment that has characterized humanity's search for meaning throughout the ages.

Origins of Freemasonry in Ancient Egypt

Ancient Egypt holds a significant place in the origins of Freemasonry, with many scholars tracing its roots back to this ancient civilization. The teachings and practices of the ancient Egyptian mystery schools are believed to have heavily influenced the development of Masonic principles.

The architectural marvels of ancient Egypt, such as the pyramids and temples, are often cited as sources of inspiration for Freemasonry. The precise craftsmanship, intricate designs, and mathematical precision found in these structures reflect the values and ideals that Freemasonry upholds. Moreover, the philosophical and spiritual beliefs of ancient Egypt, including the concepts of divine order, the immortality of the soul, and the pursuit of wisdom, resonate deeply with Masonic teachings. The reverence for knowledge, the quest for inner enlightenment, and the emphasis on moral virtue in ancient Egyptian spirituality and Freemasonry illustrate a shared commitment to personal growth and self-improvement. The ancient Egyptian reverence for symbols and allegories also parallels Masonic symbolism. The use of symbolic imagery to convey deeper meanings and esoteric truths is a common thread that connects these two traditions. Overall, the origins of Freemasonry in ancient Egypt speak to a rich tapestry of shared values, beliefs, and practices that have endured through the ages. By delving into the mysteries of this ancient civilization, Freemasons today continue to draw inspiration and guidance for their own journey toward spiritual enlightenment and moral development.

Influence of Hermeticism on Ancient Mystery Schools
Hermeticism, an ancient spiritual and philosophical tradition attributed to Hermes Trismegistus, played a significant role in shaping the beliefs and practices of the ancient mystery schools. Hermeticism's teachings emphasised the interconnectedness of all things in the universe and the quest for spiritual enlightenment through inner transformation. Central to Hermeticism is "as above, so below," which suggests that the individual's microcosm reflects the universe's macrocosm. This idea of correspondence between the physical and spiritual realms resonated deeply with the ancient mystery schools, as they believed that understanding the mysteries of the universe could lead to self-realization and spiritual evolution. Hermeticism also introduced the idea of alchemy, the process of transmuting base metals into gold, as a metaphor for the inner transformation of the individual. This symbolism of alchemy, with its emphasis on purification and refinement, became a central theme in the teachings of the ancient mystery schools, guiding initiates on their journey toward enlightenment. The principles of Hermeticism, including the pursuit of knowledge, the exploration of the spiritual dimensions of existence, and the quest for unity with the divine, heavily influenced the rituals, symbols, and philosophy of the ancient mystery schools. By incorporating Hermetic teachings into their practices, the mystery schools sought to provide initiates with a holistic understanding of the universe and themselves, paving the way for profound spiritual experiences and inner growth.

Symbolism in Ancient Mystery Schools
Symbols played a crucial role in conveying esoteric teachings and spiritual truths within the walls of ancient mystery schools.

These symbols were not merely decorative elements but held profound significance, serving as a means of transmitting hidden knowledge to the initiates. Each symbol was carefully chosen and imbued with layers of meaning that could be interpreted on various levels, depending on the depth of the seeker's understanding. One of the most prevalent symbols in ancient mystery schools was the serpent, representing wisdom, regeneration, and transformation. The shedding of the serpent's skin symbolized the cyclical nature of life and the soul's journey towards enlightenment. The serpent was also associated with dualism, embodying both the forces of good and evil. Another significant symbol was the labyrinth, a complex and intricate design that symbolized the path of initiation and self-discovery. As initiates navigated through the maze, they would face challenges and obstacles that mirrored their inner struggles and spiritual growth. The journey through the labyrinth was a metaphor for the quest for knowledge and enlightenment, with the ultimate goal being the centre, where the seeker would find unity and harmony within themselves. Geometric shapes, such as circles, triangles, and squares, also held symbolic meaning in ancient mystery schools. The circle represented eternity and unity, with no beginning or end, symbolizing the eternal cycle of life and death. The triangle symbolises the trinity of body, mind, and spirit and the three stages of initiation – purification, illumination, and perfection. The square represented stability and balance, aligning the physical and spiritual realms. In addition to these symbols, ancient mystery schools also incorporated symbolic rituals and practices into their teachings. These rituals were designed to evoke spiritual experiences, deepen the initiates' understanding of esoteric principles, and facilitate inner transformation. Through the careful use of symbols, traditions, and practices, ancient mystery schools provided a framework for initiates to explore the mysteries of the universe and uncover the hidden truths of existence.

Practices and Rituals of Ancient Mystery Schools

In the ancient mystery schools, practitioners engaged in a variety of practices and rituals aimed at spiritual growth and enlightenment. These practices were often shrouded in secrecy and symbolism, passed down through generations of initiates. One key practice in the ancient mystery schools was meditation. Initiates would frequently spend hours in deep contemplation, seeking to connect with higher realms of consciousness and unlock hidden truths about the universe and themselves. Another common practice was the use of sacred rituals and ceremonies. These rituals were performed with precision and attention to detail, often involving symbolic objects and gestures with deep spiritual significance. Initiation ceremonies were a central aspect of the mystery schools. New members would undergo elaborate rites of passage, symbolizing their entry into the inner circle of knowledge and wisdom. These ceremonies were meant to transform the individual spiritually and mark their commitment to enlightenment. Sacred dance and movement were also frequently employed in the mystery schools. Practitioners would engage in intricate choreography, often accompanied by music or chanting, to express spiritual concepts and invoke higher states of consciousness.

The mystery schools also strongly emphasised the study of ancient texts and teachings. Initiates would spend hours delving into esoteric knowledge, deciphering hidden meanings and uncovering the mysteries of the universe.

Overall, the practices and rituals of the ancient mystery schools were designed to guide individuals on a transformative journey of self-discovery and spiritual enlightenment, paving the way for the evolution of Freemasonry in the medieval era.

Transition to Medieval Stonemasonry

As ancient mystery schools gradually declined in influence during the early medieval period, a new form of organization emerged that would eventually become intertwined with the esoteric teachings of the past. This new entity was medieval stonemasonry. The transition from the secretive practices of the mystery schools to the more practical and tangible world of stonemasonry marked a significant shift in the evolution of esoteric knowledge.

Stonemasons of the medieval period were skilled artisans who constructed magnificent cathedrals, castles, and other monumental structures. These craftsmen possessed intricate knowledge of geometry, engineering, and architectural design, all passed down through apprenticeships and guild structures. It was within these guilds that the principles of ancient wisdom began to be integrated with the practical skills of the stonemason.

The Stonemasons' lodges served as centres of learning and collaboration, where members shared their knowledge and perfected their craft. Within these lodges, the traditions of the ancient mystery schools found a new home, adapting to the changing times and taking on new forms. The mystery schools' symbolic language, ritual practices, and moral virtues were woven into the fabric of medieval stonemasonry, creating a unique fusion of spiritual and practical wisdom.

As the stonemasons travelled from one construction site to another, they carried their tools, materials, and esoteric knowledge. Through their work, they transmitted the ancient teachings to future generations, ensuring that the wisdom of the past would endure. This transition period laid the foundation for the development of Freemasonry as we know it today, blending the teachings of the mystery schools with the craft of the stonemason to create a fraternity dedicated to personal growth, moral development, and brotherly love.

The Integration of Masonic Principles

As medieval stonemasonry evolved into modern Freemasonry, significant principles from ancient mystery schools were seamlessly integrated into the organisation's fabric. One fundamental principle that carried over was the emphasis on pursuing knowledge and enlightenment. Freemasonry inherited the tradition of seeking wisdom and understanding through esoteric teachings, symbolic rituals, and philosophical discussions.

Central to the integration of Masonic principles was the concept of brotherhood. Freemasonry emphasized the importance of unity, mutual support, and camaraderie among members. This sense of brotherhood transcended social boundaries and promoted inclusivity and acceptance among individuals from diverse backgrounds.

Another fundamental principle that found its way into Freemasonry was the idea of moral virtue. Ancient mystery schools strongly emphasised ethical conduct, personal integrity, and cultivating virtues such as honesty, integrity, and compassion. These same values were upheld in Freemasonry, guiding members to lead exemplary lives and contribute positively to society. Furthermore, Freemasonry integrated symbolism as a powerful tool for conveying deeper truths and spiritual insights. Just as ancient mystery schools used symbols to represent profound concepts and spiritual truths, Freemasonry employed symbols such as the square and compass, the pillars, and the apron to impart moral lessons and encourage introspection. Integrating Masonic principles from ancient mystery schools into modern Freemasonry enriched the organization with a rich heritage of wisdom, symbolism, and moral teachings. By embracing these foundational principles, Freemasonry continues to uphold the values of brotherhood, knowledge, and morality, fostering personal growth, enlightenment, and the pursuit of a virtuous life among its members.

Legacy of Ancient Mystery Schools in Freemasonry

The legacy of ancient mystery schools in Freemasonry is deeply embedded within the foundation of the craft, serving as a rich tapestry of esoteric wisdom and symbolic teachings. These ancient schools, with their sacred rituals and philosophical doctrines, laid the groundwork for the development of Freemasonry as we know it today. One of the key legacies of the ancient mystery schools in Freemasonry is the emphasis on spiritual enlightenment and self-improvement. Just as the ancient initiates sought to elevate their consciousness and attain higher levels of understanding, Freemasons strive to cultivate moral virtues, intellectual growth, and a deeper connection to the divine. The symbolic language and rituals employed in Freemasonry can be traced back to the ancient mystery traditions, where allegory and metaphor were used to convey profound truths about the nature of reality and the human experience. By drawing upon these ancient symbols and teachings, Freemasonry inspires its members to contemplate the deeper meanings of life and the universe.

Furthermore, the emphasis on initiation and ritual purification in ancient mystery schools is mirrored in the initiation ceremonies of Freemasonry. Through these rites of passage, candidates are guided on a transformative journey of self-discovery and self-mastery, mirroring the spiritual journey undertaken by initiates in the ancient mystery schools. The legacy of ancient mystery schools in Freemasonry serves as a reminder of the timeless wisdom and enduring truths passed down through the generations. By honouring and preserving these ancient teachings, Freemasonry continues to be a vessel for spiritual growth, moral development, and intellectual exploration in harmony with the noble traditions of the past.

Conclusion: Connecting the Dots

Throughout this exploration of the origins of Freemasonry in ancient mystery schools, it becomes clear that the traditions, teachings, and symbols passed down through the ages have left a lasting legacy on the craft. The intricate connections between the ancient mystery schools and Freemasonry highlight the depth of wisdom and knowledge preserved and transmitted through generations. By delving into the mythologies, rituals, and philosophical concepts of these ancient institutions, we can uncover a rich tapestry of symbolism and meaning that continues to shape the principles of Freemasonry today. The parallels between the practices of the ancient mystery schools and the principles of Freemasonry underscore a profound continuity in the pursuit of spiritual enlightenment and personal transformation. The emphasis on moral virtues, sacred geometry, and symbolic rituals bridges the ancient wisdom of the past and the modern practices of Freemasonry. Understanding this connection allows us to appreciate these teachings' timeless relevance and continued influence on the craft. By recognizing the legacy of the ancient mystery schools in Freemasonry, we are better equipped to grasp the deeper significance of the craft and its enduring impact on individuals and society. The esoteric knowledge and profound insights passed down through the centuries offer valuable lessons on morality, self-improvement, and the pursuit of wisdom. In connecting the dots between the ancient mystery schools and Freemasonry, we can trace a lineage of spiritual exploration and philosophical inquiry that inspires seekers of truth and light. As we reflect on the teachings and traditions of the ancient mystery schools, we are reminded of the importance of preserving and honouring the wisdom of our ancestors. By acknowledging the profound influence of these ancient institutions on Freemasonry, we gain a deeper understanding of the roots of the craft and the timeless truths it seeks to uphold. In bridging the gap between the past and the present, we can forge a stronger connection to the rich heritage that informs our journey toward enlightenment and self-discovery.

CHAPTER 2

Evolution of Freemasonry Among Medieval Stonemasons

Medieval stonemasons were skilled craftsmen who were crucial in constructing cathedrals, castles, and other essential structures during the Middle Ages. These craftsmen were highly respected for their expertise in working with stone and their ability to create intricate designs and structures that have stood the test of time. The origins of medieval stonemasonry can be traced back to the Roman Empire, where skilled artisans were responsible for building roads, aqueducts, and other architectural marvels. As the Roman Empire declined, the art of stonemasonry continued to be practised by craftsmen who passed down their knowledge through the centuries. During the Middle Ages, stonemasons formed guilds to regulate trade and protect their craft. These guilds established strict rules and standards for apprenticeship and training, ensuring that only highly skilled individuals could practice the craft of stonemasonry. Medieval stonemasons were responsible for building structures and creating elaborate stone carvings and sculptures that adorned buildings and served as symbols of their craftsmanship. These intricate carvings often featured religious and symbolic motifs that reflected the spiritual beliefs of the time. The work of medieval stonemasons was physically demanding and required high precision and skill. Stonemasons used simple tools such as chisels, hammers, and mallets to shape and carve stone, often working long hours in difficult conditions to complete their projects. Despite the challenging nature of their work, medieval stonemasons took great pride in their craft and were highly esteemed in society. Their contributions to architecture and art during the Middle Ages laid the foundation for the development of Freemasonry and the symbolic traditions that continue to endure.

Historical Background of Medieval Stonemasonry Guilds

The history of medieval stonemasonry guilds dates back to the early Middle Ages when skilled artisans formed associations centred around their craft. These guilds served as the foundation of the construction industry, providing a structured framework for the training and employment of stonemasons. The medieval stonemasonry guilds were instrumental in developing and preserving the specialized knowledge and skills required for constructing monumental structures such as cathedrals, castles, and bridges. Membership in these guilds was highly sought after, as it offered craftsmen a sense of community, protection, and shared identity. The guilds' hierarchical structures governed the relationships between apprentices, journeymen, and master craftsmen. Apprentices received formal training and education in the craft, starting from a young age and progressing through various levels of skill and expertise. Journeymen travelled widely to gain experience and learn different techniques. At the same time, master craftsmen oversaw the planning and execution of complex building projects. The guilds also played a crucial role in regulating working conditions, wages, and craftsmanship standards to ensure their work's quality and integrity. They enforced strict rules and codes of conduct governed by trade secrets and rituals passed down through generations. As the medieval period progressed, stonemasonry guilds evolved from purely practical and utilitarian organizations into more philosophical and symbolic institutions. This transition laid the groundwork for speculative masonry, a symbolic and philosophical approach to the craft that would later form the basis of modern Freemasonry. The historical background of medieval stonemasonry guilds is a rich tapestry of tradition, skill, and fraternity that intrigues and inspires scholars and enthusiasts. By delving into the origins and evolution of these ancient institutions, we gain a deeper appreciation for the enduring legacy of medieval stonemasons and their contributions to the built environment.

Transition from Operative to Speculative Masonry

As medieval stonemasonry guilds evolved, a significant shift occurred within the craft. This transition from operative to speculative masonry marked a turning point in the profession's history. Operative masons were practical builders who focused on the physical construction of buildings, particularly cathedrals and other structures. They honed their skills through apprenticeships and practical experience on construction sites. However, as the demand for cathedral-building waned and the

Renaissance ushered in new intellectual and cultural movements, some masons began to explore the deeper symbolic and philosophical aspects of their craft. Speculative masonry emerged as a philosophical and intellectual pursuit, focusing on the moral, ethical, and symbolic meanings behind the tools and symbols used by operative masons. This shift from operative to speculative masonry laid the foundation for modern Freemasonry, combining elements of operative and speculative traditions. It allowed masons to delve into symbolism, allegory, and moral lessons, transforming the craft into a more profound, more esoteric discipline. The transition from operative to speculative masonry blurred the lines between the practical and the philosophical, paving the way for a new era of intellectual exploration within the craft. This evolution allowed masons to transcend their role as mere builders and artisans, transforming them into keepers of ancient wisdom and seekers of spiritual enlightenment.

CHAPTER 3

Evolution of Freemasonry Among Medieval Stonemasons

Medieval stonemasons were skilled craftsmen who were crucial in constructing cathedrals, castles, and other essential structures during the Middle Ages. These craftsmen were highly respected for their expertise in working with stone and their ability to create intricate designs and structures that have stood the test of time. The origins of medieval stonemasonry can be traced back to the Roman Empire, where skilled artisans were responsible for building roads, aqueducts, and other architectural marvels. As the Roman Empire declined, the art of stonemasonry continued to be practised by craftsmen who passed down their knowledge through the centuries. During the Middle Ages, stonemasons formed guilds to regulate trade and protect their craft. These guilds established strict rules and standards for apprenticeship and training, ensuring that only highly skilled individuals could practice the craft of stonemasonry. Medieval stonemasons were responsible for building structures and creating elaborate stone carvings and sculptures that adorned buildings and served as symbols of their craftsmanship. These intricate carvings often featured religious and symbolic motifs that reflected the spiritual beliefs of the time. The work of medieval stonemasons was physically demanding and required high precision and skill. Stonemasons used simple tools such as chisels, hammers, and mallets to shape and carve stone, often working long hours in difficult conditions to complete their projects. Despite the challenging nature of their work, medieval stonemasons took great pride in their craft and were highly esteemed in society. Their contributions to architecture and art during the Middle Ages laid the foundation for the development of Freemasonry and the symbolic traditions that continue to endure.

Historical Background of Medieval Stonemasonry Guilds

The history of medieval stonemasonry guilds dates back to the early Middle Ages when skilled artisans formed associations centred around their craft. These guilds served as the foundation of the construction industry, providing a structured framework for the training and employment of stonemasons. The medieval stonemasonry guilds were instrumental in developing and preserving the specialized knowledge and skills required for constructing monumental structures such as cathedrals, castles, and bridges. Membership in these guilds was highly sought after, as it offered artisans a sense of community, protection, and shared identity. The guilds' hierarchical structures governed the relationships between apprentices, journeymen, and master artisans. Apprentices received formal training and education in the craft, starting from a young age and progressing through various levels of skill and expertise. Journeymen travelled widely to gain experience and learn different techniques. At the same time, master craftsmen oversaw the planning and execution of complex building projects. The guilds also played a crucial role in regulating working conditions, wages, and craftsmanship standards to ensure their work's quality and integrity. They enforced strict rules and codes of conduct governed by trade secrets and rituals passed down through generations. As the medieval period progressed, stonemasonry guilds evolved from purely practical and utilitarian organizations into more philosophical and symbolic institutions. This transition laid the groundwork for speculative masonry, a symbolic and intellectual approach to the craft that would later form the basis of modern Freemasonry. The historical background of medieval stonemasonry guilds is a rich tapestry of tradition, skill, and fraternity that intrigues and inspires scholars and enthusiasts. By delving into the origins and evolution of these ancient institutions, we gain a deeper appreciation for the enduring legacy of medieval stonemasons and their contributions to the built environment.

Transition from Operative to Speculative Masonry

As medieval stonemasonry guilds evolved, a significant shift occurred within the craft. This transition from operative to speculative masonry marked a turning point in the profession's history. Operative masons were practical builders who focused on the physical construction of buildings, particularly cathedrals and other structures. They honed their skills through apprenticeships and practical experience on construction sites. However, as the demand for cathedral-building waned and the

Renaissance ushered in new intellectual and cultural movements, some masons began to explore the deeper symbolic and philosophical aspects of their craft. Speculative masonry emerged as a philosophical and intellectual pursuit, focusing on the moral, ethical, and symbolic meanings behind the tools and symbols used by operative masons. This shift from operative to speculative masonry laid the foundation for modern Freemasonry, combining elements of operative and speculative traditions. It allowed masons to delve into symbolism, allegory, and moral lessons, transforming the craft into a more profound, more esoteric discipline. The transition from operative to speculative masonry blurred the lines between the practical and the philosophical, paving the way for a new era of intellectual exploration within the craft. This evolution allowed masons to transcend their role as mere builders and artisans, transforming them into keepers of ancient wisdom and seekers of spiritual enlightenment.

Development of Masonic Rituals and Symbols
The development of Masonic rituals and symbols was a gradual process that evolved alongside the transition from operative to speculative Masonry. As the craft shifted from a purely practical trade to a more philosophical and moral institution, new rituals and symbols were introduced to convey deeper meanings and teachings. One of the most essential symbols in Freemasonry is the square and compasses, which represent morality and the importance of aligning one's actions with ethical principles. The square symbolizes honesty, integrity, and fairness, while the compasses denote boundaries and self-control. Together, they remind Masons to lead a balanced and virtuous life. Another significant symbol is the letter "G," often found in the centre of the square and compasses. This symbol is interpreted in various ways, such as standing for God, geometry, or the Grand Architect of the Universe. It serves as a reminder of the spiritual aspect of Freemasonry and the importance of seeking divine guidance in one's endeavours. Masonic rituals, such as initiation ceremonies, degree conferrals, and lodge meetings, are filled with symbolism and allegory. These rituals aim to impart moral lessons, encourage personal growth, and foster a sense of brotherhood

among members. Through symbolic gestures, words, and actions, Masons learn to reflect on their virtues, values, and responsibilities in their Masonic and personal lives. Overall, the development of Masonic rituals and symbols has played a crucial role in shaping the identity and teachings of Freemasonry. By incorporating ancient traditions, sacred geometry, and moral virtues into their practices, Masons strive to uphold the timeless principles of brotherly love, relief, and truth.

Role of Medieval Stonemasons in Cathedral Construction

Medieval stonemasons were crucial in the construction of cathedrals during the Middle Ages. These skilled craftsmen were instrumental in bringing to life the grand architectural wonders that continue to awe and inspire us today. Operating within the framework of guilds, these stonemasons followed a strict hierarchical structure. They adhered to a set of rules and traditions that governed their craft. The construction of cathedrals required meticulous planning, precise execution, and unwavering dedication. Stonemasons were responsible for shaping and carving the stones that formed the intricate details of the buildings. They employed techniques passed down through generations, honing their skills to perfection. Cathedrals served as not only places of worship but also as symbols of power, wealth, and prestige. The grandeur of these structures reflected the collective efforts of countless stonemasons who dedicated their lives to their construction. Each piece of a stone laid by their hands was imbued with meaning and purpose, contributing to the overall beauty and majesty of the cathedral. The role of the medieval stonemason went beyond mere craftsmanship; it was a calling that required deep spiritual commitment and reverence for the divine. Working on these sacred buildings, they understood the importance of their work in creating spaces that inspired awe and humility in those who entered.

The legacy of medieval stonemasons lives on in the cathedrals they helped build. Their dedication to their craft, mastery of stone, and contribution to architectural history continue to be celebrated and admired to this day.

Influence of Medieval Architecture on Freemasonry

During the medieval era, the art of stonemasonry played a crucial role in constructing magnificent cathedrals and other grand structures. The intricate designs and complex architecture of these buildings served a practical purpose. They held symbolic significance for the society of that time. The meticulous craftsmanship of medieval stonemasons can still be observed in the detailed carvings, intricate patterns, and elaborate sculptures that adorn these structures. The influence of medieval architecture on Freemasonry is significant, as many of the architectural principles and design elements from this period found their way into Masonic symbolism and rituals. The use of sacred geometry, such as the golden ratio and geometric shapes, in medieval architecture is mirrored in the symbolism of Freemasonry, emphasizing harmony, balance, and unity.

Moreover, the emphasis on craftsmanship, attention to detail, and dedication to perfection that were hallmarks of medieval stonemasons are reflected in the values of Freemasonry. The commitment to moral and spiritual development, the pursuit of knowledge, and the importance of self-improvement are all principles that can be traced back to the traditions of medieval stonemasons.

By studying the architectural achievements of the medieval era, Freemasons have drawn inspiration for their rituals, symbols, and teachings. The intricate designs and hidden meanings found in medieval cathedrals have provided a rich source of symbolism and allegory for Freemasonry, helping to shape the rituals and practices of the fraternity.

In essence, the influence of medieval architecture on Freemasonry is profound, shaping the fraternity's aesthetic, philosophical, and symbolic aspects. By honouring the traditions and craftsmanship of medieval stonemasons, Freemasonry continues to uphold the values of excellence, integrity, and enlightenment passed down through the centuries.

Important Figures in Medieval Masonic History

Several key figures emerged in Masonic history throughout medieval history, shaping the trajectory of Freemasonry as we know it today. One such figure is Prince Edwin, who is said to have called together a legendary assembly of Masons at York in the 10th century. This assembly, known as the "York Grand Lodge," is considered a seminal event in the history of Freemasonry and is often cited as the starting point of organized Masonic lodges.

Another important figure in medieval Masonic history is King Athelstan of England, who is believed to have granted the first known charter to a group of stonemasons in York. This charter, known as the "Athelstan Charter," is seen as a significant milestone in the development of Freemasonry, as it provided official recognition and protection to the craft.

Additionally, the legendary figure of Hiram Abiff plays a central role in Masonic mythology, particularly in the rituals of the third degree. Hiram Abiff is portrayed as the master architect of King Solomon's Temple. He is revered for his unwavering dedication to his craft and his commitment to upholding the principles of Freemasonry.

In medieval Masonic history, these figures symbolize the dedication, skill, and tradition that have guided Freemasonry through the ages. Their stories continue to inspire Masons worldwide, reminding them of the timeless values and principles that form the foundation of the craft.

Relationship Between Medieval Stonemasons and Royalty

Medieval stonemasons held a unique and significant relationship with royalty during this period. Kings and nobility often commissioned grand architectural projects, such as castles, cathedrals, and palaces, that required the expertise of skilled stonemasons. The intricate designs and detailed craftsmanship of these structures showcased the wealth and power of the ruling elite. They served as symbols of their divine right to rule.

Royalty recognized the value of the stonemasons' knowledge and expertise, and many kings formed close ties with these craftsmen. In some cases, stonemasons were granted special privileges and exemptions from specific laws, allowing them to travel freely and work on various projects throughout the realm. These relationships helped facilitate the exchange of ideas and techniques between different regions, leading to the spread of architectural styles and Masonic traditions.

The patronage of royalty also provided stonemasons with financial stability and social standing, elevating their status within medieval society. By working on royal projects, these craftsmen gained prestige and recognition for their skills, further cementing their importance in the construction industry.

Additionally, the close relationship between medieval stonemasons and royalty often extended beyond professional collaboration. Many kings and queens were known to have personal connections to individual masons, viewing them as trusted advisors and confidants. These personal relationships not only benefited the stonemasons but also allowed them to have a voice in the political decisions of the time.

Overall, the relationship between medieval stonemasons and royalty was complex and multifaceted, encompassing professional and personal connections that helped shape the course of architectural history and the evolution of Freemasonry.

Impact of Historic Events on the Evolution of Freemasonry

Throughout history, Freemasonry has been deeply influenced by a series of pivotal events that have shaped its evolution into the modern organization we know today. One such impactful event was the Age of Enlightenment, a period marked by a renewed interest in reason, science, and intellectual inquiry. This era of intellectual enlightenment profoundly affected Freemasonry, fostering an environment where freethought and the exchange of ideas were encouraged.

Another significant historical event that left its mark on Freemasonry was the American Revolution. The ideals of liberty, equality, and fraternity that fuelled the revolution resonated deeply with Masonic principles, leading to an increased interest in Freemasonry among the United States Founding Fathers. Many prominent figures involved in the American Revolution, such as George Washington and Benjamin Franklin, were Freemasons, further solidifying the close connection between Freemasonry and the founding of the United States.

Furthermore, the Industrial Revolution in the 19th century brought about massive social and economic changes that directly impacted Freemasonry. As traditional guilds and associations faced challenges in the rapidly changing industrial landscape,

Freemasonry provided a sense of community and fraternity for individuals seeking moral and intellectual growth.

The two World Wars of the 20th century also left a lasting impact on Freemasonry. The devastation and loss of life caused by these conflicts led to a resurgence of interest in moral values and ethical principles, driving many individuals to seek solace and guidance within the Masonic Brotherhood.

In conclusion, the evolution of Freemasonry has been intricately intertwined with the unfolding of historical events throughout the centuries. These events have shaped the organization's structure and rituals and influenced its core values and guiding principles. As Freemasonry continues to adapt to the changing times, its rich history serves as a testament to the enduring legacy of the medieval stonemasons and their impact on modern Freemasonry.

Legacy of Medieval Stonemasons in Modern Freemasonry

The legacy of Medieval Stonemasons continues to shape modern Freemasonry in profound ways. The values of craftsmanship, dedication, and unity instilled in the medieval builders have been passed down through the centuries and remain central to the Masonic tradition today.

The architectural marvels created by the medieval stonemasons serve as a reminder of the importance of excellence in one's work and the enduring impact that skilled craftsmanship can have. This legacy of architectural beauty and precision is reflected in the intricate designs and symbolism found in Masonic lodges and rituals.

Furthermore, the organizational structures and traditions developed by the medieval stonemasons have had a lasting influence on the governance and operation of modern Freemasonry. The hierarchical system, the importance of mentorship and education, and the sense of brotherhood and community that defined medieval stonemason guilds are all integral aspects of contemporary Masonic lodges.

The connection between medieval stonemasonry and modern Freemasonry is historical and spiritual. The symbolic language of architecture, geometry, and moral teachings used by the medieval builders continues to be a central part of Masonic ritual and symbolism. This shared heritage creates a sense of continuity and tradition that links present-day Masons to their ancient counterparts.

In embracing the legacy of the medieval stonemasons, modern Freemasonry honours the skills and craftsmanship of those who came before and the values of integrity, excellence, and fellowship that have stood the test of time. Through maintaining this connection to their origins, Freemasons continue to draw inspiration and guidance from the rich history of their craft, ensuring that the legacy of the medieval stonemasons remains alive and vibrant in the modern Masonic tradition.

CHAPTER 4

The Symbolism of Sacred Geometry in Freemasonry
Introduction

Sacred geometry has long been a fundamental aspect of human understanding and interpretation of the world around us. From the earliest civilizations to modern-day societies, the intricate relationships between geometric shapes, numbers, and symbolism have held profound meaning and significance. In Freemasonry, sacred geometry is crucial in the rich tapestry of teachings and traditions that define this ancient craft.

The inherent beauty and harmony in geometric shapes such as circles, squares, triangles, and spirals have long been recognized as representations of divine order and balance. These shapes are not merely arbitrary constructs but are deeply rooted in the natural world and cosmic principles that govern our existence. By delving into the history of sacred geometry, we can uncover the ancient wisdom passed down through the ages and discover the timeless truths that continue to inspire and guide Freemasons in their quest for enlightenment and self-improvement.

As we embark on this journey through the annals of history, we will explore the origins of sacred geometry and its evolution across different cultures and civilizations. We will uncover the profound insights that ancient sages and scholars gleaned from studying geometric shapes and their mystical properties. By understanding the historical context in which sacred geometry arose, we can gain a deeper appreciation for its enduring significance in Freemasonry and its profound impact on the hearts and minds of those seeking to unravel its mysteries.

Join me as we unravel the intricate tapestry of sacred geometry, tracing its origins from the dawn of civilization to the present day. Through this exploration, we will unveil the hidden meanings and symbolic power within the geometric shapes that form the foundation of Freemasonry's teachings and rituals. Let us delve into the history of sacred geometry and unlock the secrets carefully preserved and passed down through generations of Masonic brethren.

History of Sacred Geometry

Sacred geometry has a rich and ancient history that dates back to the earliest civilizations. From the Egyptians and Greeks to the Romans and Renaissance thinkers, holy geometry has significantly shaped our understanding of the world around us. The study of holy geometry involves exploring the mathematical and geometric principles underlying the natural world and the universe. These principles are believed to embody fundamental truths and are often seen as expressions of divine order and harmony.

One of the earliest known examples of sacred geometry can be found in ancient Egypt, where the construction of the pyramids demonstrated a profound understanding of geometric principles. The Egyptians used geometric shapes such as circles, squares, and triangles in their architectural designs, believing they held symbolic and spiritual significance.

The Greeks also recognized the importance of geometric shapes and ratios in their philosophical and mathematical pursuits. Figures such as Pythagoras and Plato saw geometry as a pathway to understanding the universe's more profound mysteries. They believed that geometric forms represented the building blocks of creation and that these forms could be used to unlock hidden truths about the nature of reality.

During the Renaissance, scholars and artists rediscovered the teachings of the Greeks and Egyptians, leading to a revival of interest in sacred geometry. Figures such as Leonardo da Vinci and Michelangelo incorporated geometric principles into their work, believing that geometry held the key to unlocking the secrets of the cosmos.

In the following centuries, sacred geometry influenced various fields, including architecture, art, and spiritual practice. Today, the study of sacred geometry remains vital to esoteric traditions such as Freemasonry, where geometric symbols convey profound spiritual and philosophical concepts.

By exploring the history of sacred geometry, we gain a deeper appreciation for the timeless wisdom that has shaped our understanding of the world and our place within it. The study of sacred geometry invites us to contemplate the interconnectedness of all things and the universal principles that govern the cosmos.

Symbolism of Geometric Shapes

Geometric shapes are crucial in Freemasonry, serving as potent symbols that convey deep spiritual meanings. Each shape is significant, representing fundamental principles and teachings within the Masonic tradition. The use of geometric shapes in Freemasonry dates back to ancient civilizations, where these symbols reflected the divine order and harmony of the universe. By understanding the symbolism behind these shapes, Masons can gain valuable insights into the underlying principles of the craft.

The circle, with its perfect and infinite form, represents unity and eternity. It symbolizes the cyclical nature of life and the interconnectedness of all things. The square, with its four equal sides and angles, embodies stability, integrity, and truth. It serves as a reminder for Masons to live honestly and fairly.

The triangle, with its three sides and points, signifies the trinity of divinity, wisdom, and strength. It represents the balance and harmony of mind, body, and spirit. The pentagram's five points symbolize the elements of earth, water, air, fire, and spirit. It reflects the interconnectedness of the material and spiritual realms.

The hexagram, also known as the Star of David, consists of two interlocking triangles, representing the union of opposites and the balance of masculine and feminine energies. It symbolizes the integration of the spiritual and material aspects of existence. These geometric shapes are not mere symbols but tools for contemplation and meditation, guiding Masons on their spiritual growth and self-discovery journey.

In Freemasonry, the symbolism of geometric shapes serves as a visual language that transcends words, conveying profound truths that resonate with the innermost being of the initiate. By meditating on these symbols and their meanings, Masons seek to deepen their understanding of the mysteries of existence and strive to embody the virtues and values the craft upholds.

The Golden Ratio

The Golden Ratio, also known as the Divine Proportion, is a mathematical ratio that has captivated artists, architects, and philosophers for centuries. This ratio, approximately equal to

1.618, is derived from the Fibonacci sequence and is believed to convey a sense of balance, harmony, and beauty.

In sacred geometry, the Golden Ratio is a fundamental principle governing the proportions of the natural world and the universe. It is believed to reflect the divine order that underlies all creation, from the smallest atom to the vast cosmos.

In Freemasonry, the Golden Ratio holds profound symbolic significance, representing the pursuit of perfection and spiritual enlightenment. The ratio is often incorporated into Masonic architecture, artwork, and rituals to convey all existence's underlying harmony and unity.

One example of the Golden Ratio's influence in Freemasonry can be seen in the design of Masonic temples, where the proportions of columns, windows, and doorways often adhere to this ratio to create a sense of balance and harmony within the sacred space. The use of the Golden Ratio in these architectural elements is meant to evoke a sense of awe and reverence in those who enter the temple, guiding them on their journey towards self-discovery and spiritual growth.

In Masonic symbolism, the Golden Ratio is also linked to the concept of divine proportionality and the inherent order of the universe. By contemplating the beauty and complexity of this mathematical ratio, Freemasons are encouraged to recognize the interconnectedness of all things and to strive for harmony in their thoughts, actions, and relationships.

Freemasonry's Golden Ratio is a potent symbol of unity, balance, and perfection. It reminds members of the profound mysteries and truths at the heart of their ancient tradition.

The Vesica Piscis

The Vesica Piscis symbol is prominent in Freemasonry, symbolizing deeper spiritual meanings and truths within the craft. This symbol, formed by the intersection of two circles that share the same centre, represents the union of opposites and the harmony that results from their integration. In Freemasonry, the Vesica Piscis is often linked to duality and the balance of masculine and feminine energies.

Through the Vesica Piscis symbol, Freemasons are reminded of the interconnectedness of all things and the importance of finding equilibrium in all aspects of life. The symbol is also associated with the idea of creation and divine proportion, symbolizing the act of manifestation and the balance between the spiritual and material realms.

In Masonic teachings, the Vesica Piscis is often used to symbolise unity and interconnectedness among fraternity members. It represents the shared values, ideals, and goals that bind Masons together in their pursuit of moral and spiritual enlightenment. The symbol serves as a reminder of the importance of cooperation, mutual respect, and harmony in all interactions within the Masonic Brotherhood.

The Vesica Piscis also carries a sense of sacredness and mystery, inviting Freemasons to contemplate the deeper meanings and mysteries of the craft. It represents the divine order and cosmic harmony that Freemasons seek to align themselves within their personal and spiritual journeys.

Overall, the Vesica Piscis symbol in Freemasonry is a powerful reminder of the interconnected nature of the universe and the profound spiritual truths that underlie the teachings of the craft. Through its symbolism, Masons are encouraged to seek unity, harmony, and balance in all aspects of their lives, striving to embody the principles of Freemasonry in their daily actions and interactions.

The Square and Compasses

The Square and Compasses symbol is one of Freemasonry's most iconic and recognizable symbols. It consists of a square and a compass intertwined, often with the letter "G" in the centre. The square represents virtue, honesty, and morality, emphasizing the importance of living a life of integrity and truth. On the other hand, the compass symbolizes boundaries and limitations, reminding Freemasons to exercise self-control and maintain balance in their actions. When combined, the Square and Compasses symbolize the moral principles and values that Freemasons strive to uphold daily.

The symbolism of the Square and Compasses extends beyond its literal representation. It serves as a reminder for Freemasons to conduct themselves with honour and dignity, adhering to the ethical guidelines laid out by the principles of Freemasonry. The

Square and Compasses also symbolize the balance between intellect and emotion, urging Freemasons to seek harmony in their thoughts and actions.

Furthermore, the Square and Compasses symbolize the idea of building and creating, reflecting the Masonic tradition of using tools and architectural symbolism to convey moral and spiritual teachings. Just as a builder uses the square and compass to ensure precision and accuracy in construction, so too do Freemasons use these symbols to guide their journey towards self-improvement and enlightenment.

In ritualistic contexts, the Square and Compasses hold significant meaning, representing the dual responsibilities of self-discipline and moral rectitude that Freemasons are expected to uphold. Through the Square and Compasses symbolism, Freemasons are reminded of their duty to maintain the tenets of brotherly love, relief, and truth, fostering a sense of unity and fraternity within the Masonic community.

Overall, the Square and Compasses symbolize the foundational principles of Freemasonry, guiding members on their quest for personal growth, moral development, and spiritual enlightenment.

The Point Within a Circle

The Point within a Circle symbol is a significant emblem in Freemasonry, representing profound symbolism and teachings within the craft. The symbol consists of a single point enclosed within a circle, with the point symbolizing an individual Mason and the circle representing the boundaries of his duty.

In Freemasonry, the Point within a Circle symbolizes the unity of the individual Mason with the broader fraternity. It emphasizes the importance of personal integrity and ethical conduct. The central point signifies the individual's moral compass, guiding him to act in accordance with the principles of Freemasonry. The circle serves as a reminder of the boundaries within which a Mason should conduct himself, encompassing his duties to his fellow Masons, his family, and society.

The symbol also carries esoteric meanings, with the circle representing eternity and the unbroken bond that ties all Freemasons together. It signifies the everlasting nature of the teachings and traditions passed down through generations of Masons, emphasizing the timeless wisdom inherent in the craft.

Moreover, the Point within a Circle symbolizes unity and perfection within Freemasonry. Just as the point in the centre of the circle represents the individual Mason, it also symbolizes the divine spark or inner light present in each person. The circle, with its unbroken boundary, signifies the unity and harmony among Masons, irrespective of their background or beliefs.

In Masonic rituals, the Point within a Circle imparts valuable lessons on morality and brotherly love. It serves as a visual reminder for Masons to conduct themselves with honour and integrity, consistently striving to align their actions with the principles of the craft.

Overall, the Point within a Circle symbol is profoundly significant in Freemasonry, encapsulating essential teachings on unity, morality, and personal responsibility. Its timeless symbolism is a constant reminder for Masons to lead virtuous lives and uphold the principles of the craft in all their endeavours.

The Tetragrammaton

The Tetragrammaton symbol, often represented by the four Hebrew letters Yod, He, Vau, and He, holds significant importance in Freemasonry. This symbol is considered one of the most sacred in esoteric traditions. It is believed to encapsulate the divine name of God. The Tetragrammaton represents the ineffable and transcendent nature of the divine as a reminder of the divine presence in all aspects of life.

In Freemasonry, the Tetragrammaton is used as a symbol of spiritual unity and divine revelation. It is often incorporated into Masonic rituals and teachings to emphasize the importance of seeking spiritual enlightenment and understanding the deeper mysteries of existence. The Tetragrammaton's symbolic representation reinforces the interconnectedness between the individual and the cosmic order, highlighting the eternal and unchanging nature of the divine essence.

The Tetragrammaton also serves as a focal point for meditation and contemplation within Freemasonry, guiding members towards a deeper understanding of their spiritual journey. By contemplating the meaning and significance of this sacred symbol, Masons are encouraged to reflect on their connection to the divine and strive for moral and spiritual growth. The Tetragrammaton symbolizes the ultimate quest for truth, wisdom, and enlightenment, inspiring Masons to seek higher levels of understanding and consciousness.

In Freemasonry, the Tetragrammaton symbolizes the divine presence that permeates all creation and serves as a guiding light for those seeking illumination and spiritual transformation. By meditating on this sacred symbol, Freemasons are reminded of their inherent connection to the divine source and encouraged to live a life of virtue, compassion, and understanding. The Tetragrammaton symbolizes the eternal mystery and power of the divine, inviting Masons to embark on a journey of self-discovery and spiritual awakening.

Sacred Architecture

Sacred architecture plays a crucial role in Freemasonry, physically representing the spiritual principles and teachings of the craft. Masonic temples are carefully designed and constructed to embody holy geometry, with each element holding symbolic meaning. The temple layout, the rooms' proportions, and the symbols' placement create a space conducive to spiritual reflection and inner transformation.

One of the key features of Masonic architecture is the use of geometric shapes and patterns, such as the square, circle, and triangle. These shapes are not merely decorative but are imbued with deep symbolic significance, representing universal truths and principles. The careful alignment of these shapes in the temple's design reflects the harmony and order believed to govern the universe.

The use of light and shadow in Masonic architecture is also significant. Light symbolises knowledge, enlightenment, and spiritual truth, while shadow represents ignorance and darkness. The play of light and shadow within the temple space creates a sense of mystery and symbolism, inviting initiates to contemplate the contrast between knowledge and ignorance.

Masonic temples are adorned with symbolic imagery, such as the All-Seeing Eye, the Sun, Moon, Stars, and other esoteric symbols. These images serve as reminders of the higher spiritual principles that Freemasonry seeks to impart to its members. The placement of these symbols within the temple's architecture is carefully considered to enhance their impact and significance.

Overall, sacred architecture in Freemasonry is a physical structure and a vessel for spiritual transformation. Using sacred geometry, symbolism, and design principles, Masonic architecture creates a sacred space where initiates can explore the depths of their inner selves and connect with the universal truths underpinning the craft.

Conclusion

The exploration of sacred architecture within Freemasonry demonstrates the profound influence of sacred geometry on the physical structures that embody Masonic principles and teachings. Masonic temples' careful design and construction reflect a deep reverence for universal truths and spiritual symbolism. Using geometric patterns, proportions, and symbols, Masonic architecture serves as a visual representation of the inner journey of self-discovery and enlightenment that Freemasons undertake.

The sacred geometry embedded in Masonic temple architecture is not merely decorative but serves a functional and symbolic purpose. Every element is imbued with meaning and significance, from the temple's layout to the placement of specific symbols and designs. Using geometric shapes such as squares, circles, triangles, and the Golden Ratio creates a harmonious and balanced space that fosters contemplation, meditation, and spiritual growth.

Within the sacred space of a Masonic temple, members gather to engage in rituals, ceremonies, and meetings that deepen their understanding of Masonic teachings and values. The architecture becomes a silent teacher, guiding initiates through symbolic journeys of self-discovery and moral enlightenment. The sacred architecture of Freemasonry serves as a powerful reminder of the interconnectedness of the physical and spiritual realms and the timeless wisdom contained within the teachings of the Craft.

As Freemasonry continues to evolve and adapt to the modern world, sacred geometry and architectural principles remain a cornerstone of the tradition. By honouring the legacy of sacred geometry in its architectural design, Freemasonry preserves an ancient tradition that speaks to the universal truths that transcend time and culture. The sacred spaces created by Freemasons serve as a testament to the enduring power of symbolism, geometry, and spirituality in guiding individuals on their quest for self-improvement and enlightenment.

CHAPTER 5

The Influence of Hermeticism on Freemasonry

Introduction to Hermeticism

Hermeticism is an ancient spiritual and philosophical tradition that traces its roots back to the writings attributed to Hermes Trismegistus, a legendary figure believed to be a combination of the Greek god Hermes and the Egyptian god Thoth. The Hermetic texts, such as the Corpus Hermeticism, explore metaphysical concepts, spiritual practices, and esoteric knowledge.

One of the critical principles of Hermeticism is the idea of "as above, so below," which suggests a correspondence between the macrocosm (the universe) and the microcosm (the individual). This concept reflects the belief that patterns and principles observed in the natural world also exist in the spiritual realm.

Hermeticism encompasses a wide range of teachings, including astrology, alchemy, magic, and theurgy. These disciplines are seen as pathways to understanding the hidden laws of the universe and achieving spiritual enlightenment. The Hermetic tradition emphasizes the pursuit of knowledge, self-discovery, and the unity of the material and spiritual realms.

Hermeticism has influenced various philosophical and mystical traditions, including Neoplatonism, Gnosticism, and alchemy. During the Renaissance, the revival of Hermetic texts sparked a renewed interest in esoteric knowledge and mystical practices, shaping the intellectual landscape of the era.

Hermeticism's emphasis on the interconnection of the physical and spiritual worlds, the pursuit of inner wisdom, and the transformative power of knowledge continues to resonate with seekers of truth and spiritual seekers today. Hermeticism offers a unique perspective on the mysteries of existence and the nature of reality through its profound teachings and timeless wisdom.

The Origins of Hermeticism

With roots traced back to ancient Egypt, Hermeticism emerged as a philosophical and spiritual tradition emphasising the pursuit of divine wisdom and universal truths. The tradition is named after Hermes Trismegistus, a legendary figure believed to have been a fusion of the Greek god Hermes and the Egyptian god Thoth. The Corpus Hermeticism, a collection of texts attributed to Hermes Trismegistus, is a primary source of Hermetic teachings.

Hermeticism's foundational principles include the concept of "as above, so below," which highlights the interconnectedness of the macrocosm and microcosm, the universe, and the individual. This principle underscores the belief that there is harmony and correspondence between the celestial and terrestrial realms. Additionally, Hermeticism emphasizes the idea of spiritual alchemy, the inner transformation of the individual soul towards perfection and unity with the divine.

The origins of Hermeticism can be traced to the Hellenistic period, with a blend of Egyptian, Greek, and possibly Jewish influences. The writings attributed to Hermes Trismegistus were translated and studied by scholars during the Renaissance, leading to a revival of interest in Hermetic philosophy. This resurgence significantly impacted the intellectual and cultural landscape of the time, influencing prominent figures such as Marsilio Ficino, Giovanni Pico della Mirandola, and Giordano Bruno.

Hermeticism's synthesis of spiritual and philosophical ideas resonated with Renaissance thinkers seeking to reconcile ancient wisdom with Christian theology and scientific inquiry. The Hermetic texts were seen as sources of hidden knowledge that could provide insights into the nature of reality, the cosmos, and the divine. This fascination with Hermeticism contributed to developing new intellectual currents and esoteric traditions that would shape the course of Western thought.

In summary, the origins of Hermeticism lie in the ancient teachings attributed to Hermes Trismegistus, blending Egyptian, Greek, and other influences to form a rich philosophical and spiritual tradition. The revival of interest in Hermeticism during the Renaissance played a crucial role in shaping the intellectual landscape of the time and continues to inspire seekers of esoteric wisdom and universal truths.

Hermeticism's Influence on Renaissance Thinkers

During the Renaissance period, the intellectual landscape of Europe was undergoing a profound transformation. This era, known for its revival of classical learning and humanistic ideals, was also a time when the teachings of Hermeticism began to captivate the minds of scholars and thinkers. The allure of Hermeticism lay in its esoteric wisdom and emphasis on the interconnectedness of all things.

Renaissance thinkers such as Marsilio Ficino and Giovanni Pico della Mirandola were deeply influenced by Hermetic philosophy. Ficino, a renowned philosopher and translator, was pivotal in introducing Hermetic texts to the Western world. He saw Hermeticism as a way to reconcile Christian theology with the wisdom of the ancients, believing that the Hermetic teachings could lead to a deeper understanding of the divine.

Pico della Mirandola, on the other hand, was drawn to the transformative power of Hermeticism. He believed that by studying the Hermetic texts and contemplating their mysteries, individuals could elevate themselves to a higher state of consciousness and commune with the divine. Pico's Oration on the Dignity of Man reflects his belief in the unlimited potential of humanity, echoing the Hermetic idea of the microcosm reflecting the macrocosm.

The influence of Hermeticism on Renaissance thinkers extended beyond philosophical speculation. It also informed their approach to science, medicine, and alchemy. The Hermetic emphasis on the unity of the spiritual and material worlds inspired scholars to seek knowledge that could lead to the transformation and perfection of both the soul and the physical body.

In conclusion, the impact of Hermeticism on Renaissance thinkers was profound and far-reaching. It shaped their worldview, inspired their intellectual pursuits, and laid the foundation for synthesising ancient wisdom with Christian theology. The legacy of this influence can still be seen today in the enduring fascination with Hermetic philosophy and its integration into various spiritual traditions.

Hermeticism's Compatibility with Freemasonry

Hermeticism's compatibility with Freemasonry can be seen in the shared emphasis on pursuing knowledge, wisdom, and spiritual enlightenment. Both traditions strongly emphasise symbolism, allegory, and esoteric teachings to convey deeper truths about the nature of reality and the human experience. The philosophical principles found in Hermeticism, such as the concept of "as above, so below," resonate with the symbolic architecture of Freemasonry that seeks to reflect cosmic truths in microcosm.

The Renaissance thinkers who were influenced by Hermeticism also played a significant role in the development of Freemasonry, as they promoted the idea of seeking hidden knowledge and enlightenment through personal introspection and study. This intellectual climate laid the foundation for the incorporation of Hermetic principles into the rituals and teachings of Freemasonry.

The Three Hermetic Principles of Correspondence, Vibration, and Polarity align closely with Freemasonry's moral virtues and symbolic teachings. Correspondence emphasizes the interconnectedness of all things, reflecting the Masonic principle of unity and brotherhood. Vibration underscores the idea that everything in the universe vibrates at its own frequency, mirroring the concept of harmony and balance within oneself and the world. Polarity highlights the inherent duality of existence, illustrating the balance of opposing forces and the need for equilibrium in one's thoughts and actions.

The compatibility between Hermeticism and Freemasonry lies in their shared goal of personal transformation and spiritual growth. Both traditions invite individuals to explore the depths of their own nature, cultivate virtues, and strive for a higher understanding of the universe and one's place within it. The synthesis of Hermetic principles within Freemasonry enriches the experience of initiates, guiding them on a path of self-discovery, enlightenment, and moral development.

The Three Hermetic Principles: Correspondence, Vibration, Polarity

The Three Hermetic Principles: Correspondence, Vibration, Polarity

The first principle of Hermeticism is Correspondence. This principle teaches that there is a connection between all things in the universe, as above, so below. It emphasizes that everything in the physical world reflects the spiritual realms. By understanding this principle, Freemasons seek to find unity in diversity and recognize the interconnectedness of all aspects of existence.

The second principle, Vibration, posits that everything in the universe is in constant motion and vibration. This principle highlights the dynamic nature of reality and the importance of energy and frequency in shaping our experiences. Freemasons embrace this principle to understand the energetic nature of the universe and harness these vibrations for personal growth and spiritual development.

The third principle, Polarity, expounds on the concept of duality within the universe. It suggests that opposite forces are complementary and necessary for balance and harmony. Freemasons explore this principle to recognize the interplay of opposing forces in their lives and strive to find equilibrium and unity in the midst of these polarities. Embracing the three Hermetic principles deepens a Freemason's understanding of the world. It enables them to navigate life with wisdom and insight.

The Emerald Tablet of Hermes Trismegistus

The Emerald Tablet of Hermes Trismegistus is a revered text in Hermeticism and holds significant influence in Freemasonry. This ancient artefact said to contain the secrets of alchemy and the principles of the universe, is believed to be written by Hermes Trismegistus, the legendary figure who embodies the fusion of the Greek god Hermes and the Egyptian god Thoth.

The Emerald Tablet is a cryptic and enigmatic text that conveys profound wisdom about the nature of reality, the interconnectedness of all things, and the process of transformation and transmutation. One of the most famous lines from the text is "As above, so below; as below, so above," which encapsulates the concept of Correspondence - one of the Three Hermetic Principles.

The teachings of the Emerald Tablet emphasize the unity of the material and spiritual realms, the power of the mind to shape reality, and the eternal quest for spiritual enlightenment. It is said that understanding and embodying the truths hidden in the Emerald Tablet can unlock the universe's secrets and achieve inner harmony and wisdom.

In Freemasonry, the Emerald Tablet is revered as a symbol of the pursuit of knowledge and the search for truth. The Hermetic teachings in the text are reflected in Masonic rituals and symbols, showcasing the deep connection between Hermeticism and Freemasonry. The Emerald Tablet serves as a guiding light for Masons on their spiritual journey, urging them to seek enlightenment and understanding of the mysteries of the universe.

The wisdom of the Emerald Tablet continues to inspire seekers of knowledge and truth, both within the realms of Hermeticism and Freemasonry. Its timeless teachings remind us of the eternal quest for self-discovery, inner transformation, and unity with the divine. As Masons study the profound insights of Hermes Trismegistus, they are encouraged to delve deeper into the mysteries of existence and strive towards greater spiritual awareness and enlightenment.

Occult Symbols in Freemasonry

The study of Hermeticism in Freemasonry reveals a rich tapestry of symbolic imagery that holds profound meaning for initiates. These symbols bridge the esoteric teachings of Hermetic philosophy and the practical rituals of Freemasonry. One of the most prominent Hermetic symbols found within Masonic lodges is the caduceus, a staff entwined by two serpents, which symbolizes the union of opposites and the balance of forces.

The square and compass, the most recognizable symbols of Freemasonry, also have deep Hermetic significance. The square represents earthly, material concerns, while the compass signifies spiritual, celestial aspirations. Together, they embody the Hermetic principle of correspondence, the idea that the microcosm reflects the macrocosm and vice versa.

The All-Seeing Eye, often depicted in the centre of a triangle, is another Hermetic symbol that holds great importance in Freemasonry. This symbol represents divine omniscience and the eternal presence of the Great Architect of the Universe, embodying the Hermetic concept of the interconnectedness of all things.

The pillars of Jachin and Boaz, which stand at the entrance of Masonic temples, also have Hermetic connotations. Jachin symbolizes establishment and strength, while Boaz represents understanding and support. Together, they signify the balance between opposing forces and the duality present in the natural world.

These Hermetic symbols serve as guideposts for Freemasons on their journey towards enlightenment and self-discovery. By meditating on these symbols and integrating their meanings into daily life, initiates can unlock more profound layers of understanding and wisdom, connecting to the ancient mystical traditions that have influenced Freemasonry for centuries.

Alchemy and Transformation in Hermeticism and Freemasonry

Alchemy is a fundamental concept that bridges the worlds of Hermeticism and Freemasonry. Both traditions emphasize the transformative power of spiritual, mental, and physical processes to achieve a higher state of being. Alchemy aims to transmute base metals into gold, symbolizing the journey of spiritual enlightenment and self-realization.

In Hermeticism, alchemy is seen as a metaphor for the inner transformation of the alchemist, where the purification and refinement of the self lead to spiritual illumination. Similarly, Freemasonry's symbolic rituals and teachings reflect this alchemical personal growth and evolution process.

The alchemical process of purification, dissolution, and reintegration resonates deeply with the Masonic journey of self-improvement and moral development. Just as the alchemist seeks to purify and refine the raw materials to reveal their inner perfection, the Freemason strives to cultivate virtues and overcome vices to reveal their inner light.

By engaging in Freemasonry's symbolic rituals and teachings, members are encouraged to reflect on their inner alchemical journey, seeking to transmute their imperfections into virtues and wisdom. Through this transformative process, Freemasons aim to elevate themselves and contribute to the betterment of society as a whole.

Ultimately, the intersection of alchemy in Hermeticism and Freemasonry is a powerful reminder of the potential for personal growth and spiritual evolution. By embracing the alchemical principles of transformation and renewal, individuals can strive towards a higher state of being and embody the timeless wisdom of these ancient traditions.

The Influence of Hermetic Philosophy on Masonic Rituals

Hermetic philosophy has deeply influenced the rituals and practices of Freemasonry. The principles of Hermeticism, with their emphasis on inner transformation and spiritual enlightenment, resonate strongly with the core values of Freemasonry. Masonic rituals incorporate elements of alchemical symbolism and esoteric teachings, drawing on the rich tradition of Hermetic philosophy.

Within Masonic rituals, initiates are guided through a series of symbolic journeys echoing the alchemical transformation process. These rituals, filled with allegorical meanings and hidden messages, are designed to inspire self-reflection and personal growth in the individual Mason. Through the performance of these rituals, Masons are encouraged to strive for moral excellence, spiritual enlightenment, and a deeper understanding of the mysteries of existence.

Symbols and rituals in Freemasonry convey deeper truths and universal principles rooted in Hermetic philosophy. From the tracing board to the working tools, each symbol used in Masonic rituals carries layers of meaning that reflect the Hermetic concept of the interconnectedness of all things. By engaging with these symbols and participating in the rituals, Masons are encouraged to explore the depths of their own consciousness and seek a deeper understanding of the world around them.

In conclusion, the influence of Hermetic philosophy on Masonic rituals is profound and enduring. The rituals of Freemasonry are a testament to the power of symbolism and allegory in conveying timeless truths and inspiring personal transformation. Through exploring Hermetic principles within Masonic practices, Freemasons can embark on a journey of self-discovery and spiritual growth that is enriching and enlightening.

Conclusion: The Ongoing Relevance of Hermeticism in Freemasonry

Throughout history, the influence of Hermetic philosophy on Freemasonry has remained a profound and enduring force. The foundational principles of Hermeticism, with its emphasis on universal laws, spiritual transformation, and hidden knowledge, have been seamlessly woven into the fabric of Masonic teachings and rituals. The core tenets of Hermeticism, such as the principle of correspondence, have provided Freemasonry with a rich symbolic language that speaks to the interconnectedness of all things.

The ongoing relevance of Hermeticism in Freemasonry is evident in the continued use of Hermetic symbols and allegories within Masonic rituals. These symbols bridge the visible and invisible worlds, encouraging Masons to seek more profound understanding and enlightenment. Pursuing spiritual growth and self-improvement, central to Hermetic philosophy and Freemasonry, underscores the enduring connection between the two traditions.

As Freemasonry evolves and adapts to the modern world, the timeless wisdom of Hermeticism continues to offer valuable insights and guidance. The emphasis on personal responsibility, moral virtue, and the quest for inner truth resonates deeply with the core values of Freemasonry. By embracing the teachings of Hermeticism, Freemasons can cultivate a more profound sense of purpose, harmony, and unity within themselves and their communities.

In conclusion, the ongoing relevance of Hermeticism in Freemasonry is a testament to the enduring power of ancient wisdom in guiding individuals towards self-discovery and spiritual enlightenment. As Freemasons continue to uphold the traditions and principles passed down through generations, the influence of Hermetic philosophy will continue to inspire and illuminate their path towards greater understanding and fulfilment.

CHAPTER 6

The Role of Moral Virtues in Freemasonry

Introduction to Moral Philosophy in Freemasonry

Moral philosophy lies at the heart of Freemasonry, guiding its members towards a path of virtue and enlightenment. The rich tapestry of Masonic teachings emphasises moral virtues as a cornerstone of personal growth and societal harmony.

From its origins rooted in ancient traditions to its evolution among medieval stonemasons, Freemasonry has long held a deep reverence for the principles of morality. The teachings of moral philosophy in Freemasonry transcend religious and cultural boundaries, emphasizing universal values that resonate with individuals seeking to improve themselves and contribute positively to the world around them.

Through studying and contemplating moral virtues, Freemasons strive to cultivate integrity, honesty, and humility within themselves. By embracing virtues such as prudence, justice, temperance, and fortitude, Masons are encouraged to navigate life's challenges with wisdom, fairness, self-control, and courage.

The Three Theological Virtues of faith, hope, and charity hold a special significance in Freemasonry, encouraging members to cultivate a deep sense of trust in the divine, maintain optimism in adversity, and practice selfless love and compassion towards others.

As Freemasons gather in lodges to engage in ritualistic ceremonies and symbolic practices, they are reminded of the timeless wisdom embedded within the moral teachings of the Craft. Through their dedication to upholding moral virtues, Freemasons strive to foster a sense of brotherly love, unity, and mutual respect within their communities.

The introduction to moral philosophy in Freemasonry serves as a guiding light for members on their journey of self-discovery and moral enlightenment. By embracing the timeless principles of virtue and ethics, Freemasons seek to lead lives of purpose, integrity, and moral excellence, embodying the noble ideals of the Craft in their daily interactions and endeavours.

Historical Perspective on Moral Virtues in Masonic Traditions

Throughout history, moral virtues have played a significant role in shaping the principles and teachings of Freemasonry. The ethical foundations of Freemasonry can be traced back to ancient civilizations and the philosophical traditions that influenced the development of the craft. Greek and Roman thinkers emphasized the importance of moral virtues such as wisdom, justice, courage, and moderation, which are also central to Masonic teachings.

In the medieval period, the concept of moral virtues was further developed within the guild system, which laid the groundwork for the ethical framework of Freemasonry. Operative masons, responsible for constructing cathedrals and other sacred buildings, were expected to adhere to strict moral and ethical standards. These principles of honesty, integrity, and mutual respect were passed down through the generations. They formed the basis of the moral virtues upheld by Freemasons today.

As Freemasonry evolved in the early modern period, the teachings of moral philosophy became more explicitly incorporated into the rituals and symbolism of the craft. The Four Cardinal Virtues - prudence, justice, temperance, and fortitude - became central pillars of Masonic teachings, representing the essential qualities that a Mason should strive to cultivate in his personal and professional life.

The historical perspective on moral virtues in Masonic traditions demonstrates the enduring importance of ethical values and principles in Freemasonry. By embracing these virtues and upholding the moral standards set forth by the craft, Freemasons not only strengthen their own character but also contribute to the betterment of society.

In the next section, we will explore in more detail the significance of the Four Cardinal Virtues in Freemasonry and how they shape the moral compass of Masonic brethren.

The Four Cardinal Virtues: Prudence, Justice, Temperance, and Fortitude

Prudence is a cardinal virtue highly esteemed within the Masonic tradition. It emphasizes the importance of cautious decision-making and thoughtful consideration before taking action. In Freemasonry, prudence is a guiding principle that helps individuals navigate life's challenges and make wise choices that benefit themselves and others.

Justice is another cardinal virtue that holds significant importance in Freemasonry. It represents fairness, equity, and adherence to moral principles. Masons are encouraged to uphold justice in their interactions with others, seek truth, and ensure their actions are guided by ethical standards.

Temperance is a virtue that focuses on self-control, moderation, and balance in all aspects of life. In Freemasonry, temperance is emphasized to achieve harmony within oneself and in relationships. By practising temperance, individuals can avoid excesses and maintain a disciplined approach to their thoughts, words, and actions.

Fortitude is the fourth cardinal virtue in Freemasonry, symbolizing courage, strength, and resilience in the face of adversity. Masons are urged to cultivate inner fortitude to withstand challenges, persevere in difficult times, and uphold their values and beliefs. By embodying fortitude, individuals can demonstrate bravery and steadfastness in pursuing their Masonic journey.

Incorporating the teachings of the four cardinal virtues - prudence, justice, temperance, and fortitude - Freemasonry seeks to instil a moral framework that guides members towards becoming better individuals and contributing positively to society. These virtues are pillars of strength in the Masonic journey, fostering personal growth, ethical conduct, and a commitment to upholding timeless principles of virtue and integrity in all endeavours.

The Three Theological Virtues: Faith, Hope, and Charity
The Three Theological Virtues: Faith, Hope, and Charity

Faith, hope, and charity are revered as the three theological virtues within Freemasonry, holding a significant place within the moral fabric of the organization. Faith is the foundation upon which a Mason builds his spiritual beliefs and understanding of the world. It represents a steadfast trust in a higher power and a belief in the universe's divine order.

Hope is the virtue that sustains a Mason through challenging times, providing a sense of optimism and resilience in the face of adversity. It inspires individuals to look towards the future with positivity and anticipation, knowing that better days lie ahead.

Often considered the greatest of the virtues, Charity embodies the spirit of selflessness and compassion that Freemasons are encouraged to cultivate. It extends beyond mere acts of giving to encompass a mindset of generosity, kindness, and understanding towards all beings.

These three theological virtues form a trinity of spiritual principles that guide Masons' personal growth and interactions with others. They remind individuals of the importance of maintaining a strong faith, nurturing hope in times of trouble, and practising charity towards those in need. By embodying these virtues daily, Freemasons strive to create a more harmonious and benevolent world rooted in the values of faith, hope, and charity.

The Masonic Emphasis on Brotherly Love and Fraternal Affection

Brotherly love and fraternal affection are fundamental principles in Freemasonry, emphasizing the importance of unity and solidarity among its members. Within the Masonic community, a bond exists that transcends differences and fosters a sense of true brotherhood. This principle is rooted in the belief that all individuals, regardless of background or status, are equal and deserving of respect.

Members of the fraternity are encouraged to treat each other with kindness, compassion, and understanding, embodying the values of tolerance and acceptance. Through charity, support, and guidance, Masons demonstrate their commitment to one another and society's collective welfare.

The concept of brotherly love extends beyond mere words or gestures; it represents a deep-seated bond that unites individuals in a shared pursuit of moral and spiritual growth. By embracing this principle, Freemasons create a supportive environment where mutual trust and friendship flourish, enabling each member to thrive personally and contribute meaningfully to the fraternity.

Through brotherly love and fraternal affection, Freemasonry seeks to instil a profound sense of interconnectedness and shared responsibility in its members. This guiding principle serves as a reminder of the importance of compassion, empathy, and solidarity in building a harmonious and enlightened society.

Understanding the Importance of Integrity and Honesty in Masonic Ideals

Integrity and honesty are two cornerstones of the Masonic ideals. Within Freemasonry, members are expected to uphold the highest ethical standards and demonstrate integrity in all their actions. Honesty is valued not only in dealings with others but also in being true to oneself. By embodying these virtues, Freemasons strive to create a community built on trust and respect.

In Freemasonry, integrity entails being true to one's word, acting sincerely, and maintaining a strong moral character. Freemasons are encouraged to cultivate integrity in their personal and professional lives, serving as a beacon of moral virtue for others to follow. By embracing integrity, members of the fraternity demonstrate their commitment to upholding the principles of Freemasonry and contributing positively to society.

Honesty, another fundamental value within Freemasonry, goes hand in hand with integrity. Freemasons are expected to be truthful in their interactions, transparent in their dealings, and genuine in their intentions. By fostering a culture of honesty, Freemasonry fosters an environment of openness and trust where members can engage in meaningful dialogue and collaboration.

The importance of integrity and honesty in Masonic ideals extends beyond individual behaviour to the broader impact on the fraternity. By upholding these values, Freemasons not only strengthened their bond as brothers but also enhanced the reputation of Freemasonry in the eyes of the public. Integrity and honesty serve as the foundation upon which the principles of Freemasonry are built, guiding members in their pursuit of personal growth, moral development, and service to others.

In practising integrity and honesty, Freemasons demonstrate their commitment to living by a higher ethical standard and contribute to the collective pursuit of truth, justice, and enlightenment. Through their actions and conduct, members of the fraternity exemplify the principles of Freemasonry and uphold the legacy of honour and integrity passed down through generations of Masons.

By embracing integrity and honesty as core values, Freemasons embody what it means to be a Mason and contribute to the legacy of brotherhood, wisdom, and enlightenment that defines the Masonic tradition.

The Role of Diligence and Industriousness in Masonic Work

In Freemasonry, the principles of diligence and industriousness form the cornerstone of the Masonic work ethic. Masons are encouraged to approach their tasks with dedication, commitment, and a strong work ethic. The value of hard work and perseverance is emphasized throughout Masonic teachings, reflecting the importance of diligence in achieving personal growth and contributing to the greater good of society.

Members of the Masonic fraternity are expected to apply themselves wholeheartedly to their duties, whether within the Lodge or in their daily lives. By embodying the virtues of diligence and perseverance, Masons fulfilled their responsibilities with excellence and set an example for others to follow. Through their focused effort and unwavering dedication, Masons strive to uphold the values of integrity and accountability in all aspects of their endeavours.

Diligence in Masonic work entails meticulous attention to detail and a willingness to put in the necessary time and effort to succeed. Masons are encouraged to approach tasks with a sense of purpose and a commitment to excellence, recognizing that thoroughness and precision are essential in upholding the standards of the Craft. By cultivating a spirit of diligence in their work, Masons seek to honour the traditions of Freemasonry and contribute positively to the community around them.

Industriousness, on the other hand, embodies the idea of sustained effort and productivity in all undertakings. Masons are urged to be proactive, resourceful, and diligent in their pursuits, demonstrating a willingness to work hard and persevere in facing challenges. By embracing a mindset of diligence, Masons strive for personal advancement and actively engage in activities that promote the welfare of others and enrich the Masonic Brotherhood as a whole.

In the context of Masonic practice, diligence and industriousness are guiding principles that inspire Masons to work diligently towards self-improvement and the betterment of society. By upholding these values, Masons demonstrate their commitment to excellence, integrity, and service, embodying the enduring legacy of Freemasonry as a beacon of moral and ethical conduct in a world that values hard work, dedication, and persistence.

Exploring the Virtue of Humility and its Significance in Masonic Practice

Humility is a cornerstone virtue in Freemasonry, embodying the essence of personal modesty and selflessness. It is a quality that encourages individuals to recognize their limitations, show respect for others, and approach life with humility and modesty. In Masonic practice, humility significantly fosters a harmonious and respectful environment among its members.

Within Freemasonry, humility is not viewed as a sign of weakness but rather as a strength that enables individuals to embrace their vulnerabilities and learn from their experiences. By practising humility, Masons cultivate a sense of inner peace and acceptance, which allows them to interact with others in a spirit of humility and mutual understanding.

Humility in Masonic practice extends beyond mere words and gestures; it is reflected in the actions and behaviours of members as they work together towards common goals. By demonstrating humility in their daily interactions, Masons uphold the values of unity, harmony, and cooperation within the fraternity.

The significance of humility is also evident in Masonic rituals and symbols, which serve as powerful reminders of its importance in the journey of self-improvement. Masons are encouraged to embrace humility as a guiding principle in pursuing moral and spiritual growth through ritualistic practices and symbolic representations.

In essence, exploring the virtue of humility in Masonic practice is a transformative experience that shapes individuals into compassionate, empathetic, and genuine beings. By embodying the qualities of humility, Masons not only enhance their personal development but also contribute to the collective well-being of the fraternity as a whole.

How Masonic Rituals and Symbols Reinforce Moral Virtues

Masonic rituals and symbols are crucial in reinforcing moral virtues within the fraternity. Members are guided towards a deeper understanding and embodiment of ethical principles through the allegorical teachings and symbolic representations of Masonic ceremonies. The use of rituals, with their structured sequences and symbolic actions, imprints moral lessons in the participants' minds, leading to introspection and self-improvement.

The various symbols employed in Freemasonry, such as the square, compass, and the working tools of the operative mason, carry profound meanings that encourage members to uphold moral values daily. These symbols remind Masons of the importance of integrity, honesty, and humility, guiding them on their journey towards moral excellence.

By partaking in Masonic rituals and meditating on the symbolic messages they convey, members are inspired to translate these teachings into action. The repetition and reinforcement of these rituals and symbols help instil moral virtues within individuals, nurturing a sense of moral responsibility and ethical conduct within the fraternity and the broader community.

Ultimately, the ongoing practice of reflecting on Masonic rituals and symbols serves as a continuous reminder for members to uphold the moral virtues that lie at the core of Freemasonry. Through this engagement with ritualistic practices and symbolic representations, Masons can deepen their understanding of moral principles and strive towards personal and collective moral growth.

Conclusion: The Ongoing Practice of Moral Virtues in Freemasonry

Freemasonry upholds a tradition that strongly emphasises the practice of moral virtues. Through the intricate system of rituals and symbols, Freemasonry instils in its members the values of integrity, honesty, humility, and diligence. These moral virtues are not merely abstract concepts but are lived out in the daily lives of Masons. Freemasons strive to uphold the highest ethical standards in all their lives by continuously integrating these virtues into their actions and interactions.

The ongoing practice of moral virtues in Freemasonry guides members, encouraging them to embody brotherly love, charity, and mutual support. This daily commitment to moral excellence fosters a sense of unity and camaraderie among Masons, creating a supportive community where individuals can grow and evolve on their journey towards self-improvement.

Through the practice of moral virtues, Freemasonry transcends mere philosophical discourse and transforms into a way of life. By upholding the principles of prudence, justice, temperance, fortitude, faith, hope, and charity, Masons strive to make meaningful contributions to their communities and society at large. Committing to moral virtues is not a static concept but an ongoing process of self-reflection, growth, and service to others.

As Freemasons continue to uphold the ideals of moral virtues in their daily lives, they contribute to the legacy of a timeless tradition that seeks to build a better world through ethical living and compassionate action. The ongoing practice of moral virtues in Freemasonry is a testament to the enduring relevance of these foundational principles in a rapidly changing world, emphasizing the importance of integrity, compassion, and service as essential pillars of a meaningful and purposeful life.

CHAPTER 7

The Masonic Initiation Rituals

Introduction to Initiation Rituals in Freemasonry

Initiation rituals are at the heart of Freemasonry, serving as a sacred and symbolic journey that every member must undertake. These rituals hold deep significance within the Masonic tradition, with roots that stretch back through the annals of history. By delving into the rich tapestry of Masonic initiation rituals, we can better understand the traditions, symbols, and values that define this ancient brotherhood.

The initiation process in Freemasonry is a carefully structured and ritualistic experience that marks the beginning of a member's journey into the mysteries and teachings of the Craft. It is a transformative experience that symbolizes rebirth, growth, and enlightenment. Through the initiation rituals, new members are welcomed into the Masonic family and guided on a moral and spiritual development path.

Historically, Masonic initiation rituals can be traced back to the ancient guilds and stonemason traditions of medieval Europe. These early rituals were designed to impart knowledge, skills, and values to apprentices as they progressed through the ranks of the craft. Over time, these rituals evolved and were adapted to reflect the spiritual and philosophical teachings that underpin Freemasonry today.

The initiation rituals in Freemasonry blend symbolism, allegory, and moral lessons. Each aspect of the ritual has a deeper meaning intended to guide the candidate on their journey of self-discovery and self-improvement. From the symbolic use of tools and symbols to reciting oaths and obligations, every element of the initiation ritual has a purpose and significance that contributes to the overall experience.

In modern Freemasonry, the initiation rituals continue to play a central role in the initiation process. They serve as a rite of passage, marking a candidate's transition from an outsider to an initiated fraternity member. The experience of undergoing the initiation rituals can be challenging, enlightening, and transformative, leaving a lasting impact on the individual's life and character.

As we explore the intricacies of Masonic initiation rituals, we will uncover the hidden meanings and teachings beneath the surface. By understanding the importance of these rituals, we can gain a deeper appreciation for the traditions and values that have shaped Freemasonry for centuries.

Historical Origins of Masonic Initiation Rituals

The roots of Masonic initiation rituals can be traced back to ancient mystery schools emphasising the importance of spiritual enlightenment and self-discovery. These schools were known for their esoteric teachings and initiation ceremonies, which sought to impart hidden knowledge and wisdom to their students.

Over time, these traditions evolved and were passed down through various cultures and civilizations, eventually finding their way into the practices of medieval stonemasons. The stonemasons, responsible for constructing cathedrals and other monumental buildings, developed unique initiation rituals infused with symbolism and sacred meaning.

Freemasonry emerged as a formal organization in the early modern period, so it incorporated these ancient traditions and rituals into its structure. The historical origins of Masonic initiation rituals reflect a blend of ancient wisdom, medieval craftsmanship, and Enlightenment ideals.

The rituals are steeped in symbolism and allegory, drawing on themes of death and rebirth, light and darkness, and the journey from ignorance to enlightenment. Each step of the initiation process is carefully designed to convey moral lessons and philosophical truths to the candidate.

By understanding the historical origins of Masonic initiation rituals, we gain insight into the rich tapestry of symbolism and tradition that continues to shape the experiences of Freemasons today. These rituals serve as a bridge between the past and the present, connecting initiates to a legacy of ancient wisdom and profound teachings.

Symbolism and Significance of Initiation Ceremonies

Symbolism and Significance of Initiation Ceremonies

Initiation ceremonies in Freemasonry hold profound symbolism and significance, deeply rooted in tradition and esoteric teachings. These rituals serve as transformative experiences for candidates, guiding them on a journey of self-discovery and enlightenment.

Central to the symbolism of Masonic initiation ceremonies is rebirth and spiritual awakening. As they progress through the degrees, candidates are metaphorically reborn through symbolic gestures, words, and actions. This process represents a symbolic death of the old self and the emergence of a new, enlightened individual committed to the principles of Freemasonry.

The initiation ceremonies also emphasize the importance of knowledge, wisdom, and self-improvement. Candidates are encouraged to seek truth, broaden their understanding of moral virtues, and strive for personal growth and development. By undergoing these rites of passage, individuals are challenged to reflect on their values, beliefs, and actions, paving the way for moral and intellectual enlightenment.

Furthermore, the symbols and rituals used in Masonic initiation ceremonies are rich in allegorical meaning, drawing on ancient traditions, mythologies, and universal principles. From the symbols of the tools of the trade to the architectural references, each element conveys profound lessons about morality, brotherhood, and the pursuit of truth.

Ultimately, the significance of Masonic initiation ceremonies lies in their ability to foster a sense of camaraderie, mutual respect, and shared values among Freemasons. By experiencing these rites together, initiates form bonds of brotherhood that transcend individual differences and unite them in a quest for spiritual enlightenment and moral excellence.

The Three Degrees of Freemasonry: Entered Apprentice, Fellowcraft, Master Mason

The Three Degrees of Freemasonry - Entered Apprentice, Fellowcraft, Master Mason

The three degrees of Freemasonry - Entered Apprentice, Fellowcraft, and Master Mason - form the core structure of the Masonic initiation system. Each degree represents a personal and spiritual development, leading the candidate through self-discovery and moral growth.

The Entered Apprentice degree marks the beginning of the candidate's initiation into Freemasonry. Symbolically, it represents the birth of new knowledge and enlightenment. During this stage, the candidate learns the fundamental teachings of the Craft, receives the symbolic tools of the trade, and is introduced to the foundational principles of morality and brotherly love.

Advancing to the Fellowcraft degree signifies a deeper level of understanding and commitment. The Fellowcraft is tasked with further exploration of the symbolic teachings of Freemasonry, particularly focusing on the concepts of education, knowledge, and intellectual enlightenment. This degree emphasizes the importance of self-improvement and the pursuit of wisdom.

Reaching the Master Mason degree is the culmination of the candidate's journey through the Masonic initiation process. It represents the attainment of mastery and full membership within the Craft. The Master Mason degree delves into profound philosophical and moral lessons, guiding the individual towards a deeper comprehension of the principles of Freemasonry and the responsibilities of brotherhood.

Each of the three degrees of Freemasonry builds upon the previous one, providing a comprehensive curriculum for spiritual and moral development. By progressing through these stages, initiates gain a greater understanding of themselves, their place in the world, and their duty to uphold the values of Freemasonry.

Preparation and Prerequisites for Initiation

Potential candidates for initiation into Freemasonry must meet specific requirements and follow a prescribed process before being accepted into the fraternity's ranks. One key prerequisite is the individual's belief in a higher power, as Freemasonry emphasizes spirituality and moral values. Applicants must also be of good character, with a reputation for honesty, integrity, and upright conduct.

Once a candidate expresses interest in joining Freemasonry, they typically undergo a series of interviews with existing members of the lodge. These interviews allow both parties to get to know each other and ensure a good fit within the fraternity. During this time, the candidate can ask questions and learn more about Freemasonry's principles and teachings.

Candidates are encouraged to familiarize themselves with the fraternity's history, symbols, and rituals before initiation. This preparation helps individuals understand Freemasonry's traditions and values, allowing them to approach the initiation process with respect and reverence.

Additionally, candidates must commit to upholding Freemasonry's moral standards and ethical principles. This includes a dedication to personal growth, self-improvement, and the betterment of society. By demonstrating a willingness to embody these ideals, candidates show readiness to become a Freemason.

Overall, the preparation and prerequisites for initiation into Freemasonry underscore the importance of commitment, character, and a sincere desire to seek knowledge and wisdom. By meeting these requirements, candidates lay the foundation for a meaningful and enriching experience within the fraternity.

The Layout and Setup of the Lodge for Initiation

The Masonic Lodge is meticulously arranged to create a solemn and sacred ambience conducive to the initiation ceremony. The layout of the lodge plays a crucial role in setting the tone and atmosphere for the rituals that will take place within its walls. The lodge is typically a rectangular room, symbolizing the earthly plane, with an altar at its centre, representing the focal point of spiritual connection.

The lodge room is adorned with symbolic decorations, such as the tracing boards and the Master's carpet, which are visual aids for conveying more profound philosophical teachings to the candidates. The layout includes the Three Great Lights of Freemasonry – the Volume of the Sacred Law, the Square, and the Compasses – positioned in a prominent place to emphasize their importance in guiding a Freemason's conduct.

The seating arrangement within the lodge is also significant, with designated seating for various officers and members based on their ranks and roles in the ceremony. The candidate is positioned in a specific spot, symbolizing their journey from darkness to light. At the same time, the Worshipful Master sits in the East, representing wisdom, enlightenment, and leadership.

The lodge room is illuminated by candles or lights, symbolizing the search for knowledge and enlightenment. The layout and setup of the lodge create a sacred space where the initiates can experience a profound sense of solemnity, symbolism, and spirituality as they undertake their journey through the rituals of Freemasonry.

The Role of Ritual Elements: Tools, Symbols, and Oaths

The ritual elements used in Freemasonry play a crucial role in conveying deeper meanings and teachings to initiates. Tools, symbols, and oaths are fundamental aspects of Masonic ceremonies, each carrying significant symbolism and serving a specific purpose in the initiation process.

Tools such as the square, compass, plumb line, and trowel are emblematic of moral virtues and principles that Masons are encouraged to uphold daily. The square represents integrity and honesty, reminding members to act fairly and truthfully. The compass signifies restraint and boundaries, urging individuals to maintain balance and moderation in their actions. The plumb line symbolizes uprightness and moral rectitude, guiding Masons to lead upright and virtuous lives. The trowel represents unity and harmony, emphasizing the importance of building strong and supportive relationships within the Masonic community.

Symbols are profoundly significant in Freemasonry, serving as visual representations of abstract concepts and philosophical truths. Each symbol is rich in meaning and can be interpreted on multiple levels, providing initiates with a framework for moral and spiritual reflection. From the blazing star to the beehive, from the rough ashlar to the tracing board, each symbol conveys a unique message that contributes to the overall philosophical teachings of the Craft.

Oaths are a solemn commitment made by initiates during their initiation rituals, binding them to the principles and values of Freemasonry. These oaths serve as a symbolic gesture of dedication and loyalty to the Craft, reinforcing the importance of upholding the teachings and traditions of the fraternity. By taking these vows, individuals commit to living by Freemasonry's moral and ethical standards, holding themselves accountable to the principles of brotherly love, relief, and truth.

In conclusion, the ritual elements of tools, symbols, and oaths are essential to Masonic initiation ceremonies. They impart moral lessons, guide spiritual reflection, and deepen the understanding of the philosophical teachings of Freemasonry. Through these symbolic elements, initiates are called to embody the values and principles of the Craft, ensuring a lifelong commitment to personal growth, moral excellence, and fraternal fellowship.

The Spiritual and Philosophical Dimensions of Initiation

Within Freemasonry, the initiation process serves as a gateway to the spiritual and philosophical dimensions of the craft. It is a transformative journey that transcends the physical realm and delves into the individual's psyche and soul.

During the initiation ceremony, the candidate is symbolically reborn, shedding their former self and embracing a new identity as a Freemason. This initiation process mirrors the alchemical concept of transformation and purification, where base elements are transmuted into spiritual gold.

The rituals and symbols used in the initiation ceremony are not merely empty gestures but are imbued with deep esoteric meanings that convey profound philosophical truths. The operative mason's tools, such as the square, compass, and plumb, are symbols of moral and spiritual guidance, urging the candidate to strive for perfection in their actions and thoughts.

Central to the spiritual dimension of initiation is the concept of light. Freemasonry teaches that the search for light is a metaphor for pursuing truth, knowledge, and enlightenment. Through the initiation process, the candidate embarks on a quest for inner illumination, seeking to uncover the hidden truths of existence and the mysteries of the universe.

The philosophical dimensions of initiation are reflected in the teachings and lectures that accompany each degree. These lessons delve into moral virtues, ethical principles, and universal truths that guide the Freemasons toward self-improvement and enlightenment. By contemplating these teachings, the initiate gains a deeper understanding of themselves, their place in the world, and their connection to the divine.

Ultimately, the spiritual and philosophical dimensions of initiation in Freemasonry provide a framework for personal growth, introspection, and spiritual development. The journey through the degrees is not merely a ritualistic exercise but a profound experience that challenges, inspires, and transforms individuals, leading them toward self-discovery and enlightenment.

The Moral Lessons Taught Through Initiation

Freemasonry is deeply rooted in the teachings of moral virtues and values, which are imparted to candidates through initiation. The initiation rituals serve as a transformative experience, guiding individuals toward self-discovery and moral enlightenment.

Through the symbolic rites and allegorical lessons of Freemasonry, candidates are reminded of the importance of moral integrity, honesty, and ethical conduct in their daily lives. The rituals emphasize the significance of virtues such as compassion, charity, truthfulness, and integrity, encouraging members to uphold these values in all their actions and interactions with others.

One of the key moral lessons taught through Masonic initiation is the concept of equality and unity among all individuals, regardless of their background or social status. By going through the initiation rituals, candidates learn to respect and value the inherent worth of every human being, fostering a sense of brotherhood and camaraderie within the Masonic community.

Furthermore, the initiation rituals highlight the importance of self-improvement and personal growth. Candidates are encouraged to reflect on their own strengths and weaknesses, seeking to cultivate positive traits and overcome shortcomings. The journey of initiation challenges individuals to strive for excellence in all aspects of their lives, inspiring them to become better versions of themselves and contribute positively to society.

Overall, the moral lessons taught through Masonic initiation are aimed at instilling a sense of duty, honour, and responsibility in members, guiding them to lead moral and meaningful lives guided by the timeless values of Freemasonry.

The Impact of Initiation Rituals on Freemasons' Personal Growth and Development

Masonic initiation rituals are crucial to Freemasons' personal growth and development. These rituals serve as a transformative experience, guiding individuals on a profound journey of self-discovery and moral reflection. Freemasons are presented with valuable lessons and teachings that impact their character and outlook on life through the structured and symbolic nature of the initiation ceremonies.

The rigorous initiation process challenges individuals to confront their beliefs, values, and principles. The rituals instil a sense of responsibility and accountability in Freemasons by requiring candidates to take oaths and make solemn commitments. This fosters a deep understanding of integrity and honour that becomes central to their personal and professional lives.

Moreover, the symbolism embedded within the initiation rituals inspires contemplation and introspection. Symbolic tools, gestures, and actions during the ceremonies encourage Freemasons to reflect on the deeper meaning behind their actions and intentions. This metaphorical language catalyses personal growth and spiritual understanding, prompting individuals to strive for higher ideals and virtues.

The emotional and psychological impact of the initiation rituals cannot be understated. The solemnity and solemnity of the ceremonies evokes potent emotions and stirs the candidates' souls. This emotional experience catalyses personal transformation, helping individuals break down barriers and limitations to achieve higher consciousness and self-awareness.

In conclusion, the impact of initiation rituals on Freemasons' personal growth and development is profound and enduring. Through these transformative experiences, individuals can cultivate a solid moral compass, deepen their understanding of themselves and the world around them, and strive towards becoming better versions of themselves. The lessons learned during initiation rituals become integral to Freemasons' personal and spiritual journey, guiding them on a path of continuous self-improvement and enlightenment.

CHAPTER 8

The Secret Teachings of Freemasonry
Introduction to Esoteric Knowledge

Esoteric knowledge lies at the heart of Freemasonry, shrouded in mystery and secrecy. The hidden wisdom has been passed down through generations of Masons, guiding them on a journey of self-discovery and enlightenment. Within the sacred teachings of Freemasonry, there are depths of understanding that go beyond the surface rituals and symbols. This esoteric knowledge unlocks the keys to unlocking the true nature of reality and the divine purpose of each individual Mason.

Pursuing esoteric knowledge is not simply an intellectual exercise but a spiritual quest for truth and self-transformation. It requires a willingness to delve into the hidden meanings behind symbols and texts, contemplate the mysteries of the universe, and seek a deeper understanding of the self. Through the study of esoteric knowledge, Masons learns to see beyond the material world and connect with the spiritual truths that underlie all existence.

Central to the Masonic tradition is the idea that wisdom is a sacred gift that must be earned through study, contemplation, and self-reflection. Esoteric knowledge is not simply handed down from teacher to student. Still, it must be actively sought and internalized through personal effort and dedication. It is a path of initiation and illumination, leading Mason to self-discovery and moral growth.

The secrets of Freemasonry are not meant to be hidden indefinitely but to be revealed to those who are ready to receive them. As Masons progress through their degrees and rituals, they are gradually initiated into deeper levels of understanding and wisdom. Esoteric knowledge is not a destination but a continual journey of learning and enlightenment, guiding Masons towards a greater awareness of themselves, their place in the world, and their connection to the divine.

In pursuing esoteric knowledge, Masons are encouraged to question, seek, and explore the mysteries of the Craft. Freemasonry's true secrets are revealed through seeking, transforming the individual Mason and shaping them into a wiser, more enlightened being. Esoteric knowledge is not a static body of information but a living tradition that continues to evolve and inspire Masons on their quest for truth and understanding.

The Five Points of Fellowship

The Five Points of Fellowship is a sacred gesture within Freemasonry that holds profound symbolic significance. It represents the unity and brotherhood shared among Masons, transcending physical boundaries to connect on a deeper spiritual level. This ritual involves touching five points on the body - foot to foot, knee to knee, breast to breast, hand to back, and cheek to cheek - symbolizing the bonds of fidelity, trust, and mutual support that unite Masons in their collective pursuit of enlightenment. Through this act, Masons reaffirm their commitment to upholding the principles of the Craft and supporting one another in their shared quest for moral and spiritual growth. The Five Points of Fellowship is a powerful reminder of the interconnectedness and solidarity that characterize the Masonic brotherhood, fostering a sense of kinship and camaraderie that transcends individual differences and fosters a sense of unity among members.

The Lost Word

The concept of the Lost Word holds a profound significance within the esoteric teachings of Freemasonry. It represents the eternal quest for spiritual enlightenment and the ultimate pursuit of truth. The Lost Word is a symbol of hidden knowledge, a sacred wisdom that lies beyond the grasp of ordinary understanding. Within the Masonic tradition, the search for the Lost Word is a metaphor for the journey of self-discovery and inner transformation. It symbolizes the eternal pursuit of light and wisdom, guiding the Mason towards enlightenment and self-realization.

The quest for the Lost Word is a central Masonic ritual and symbolic theme. It represents the eternal mystery of existence and the search for ultimate truth. As Masons progress in their journey through the Craft, they are encouraged to seek the Lost Word within themselves, to unlock the hidden wisdom that lies dormant within their souls. Pursuing the Lost Word is not just a search for knowledge but a transformative process that leads to spiritual growth and enlightenment.

The Lost Word also serves as a reminder of the power of language and communication. In the Masonic tradition, words are imbued with symbolic meaning and carry a more profound significance beyond their literal interpretation. The search for the Lost Word challenges Masons to reflect on the power of language and the importance of using words wisely. By seeking the Lost Word, Masons are reminded of the sacred nature of language and the need to communicate with truth, integrity, and respect.

Ultimately, the quest for the Lost Word is a deeply personal journey that each Mason must undertake in their own way. It is a journey of self-discovery, introspection, and contemplation. By seeking the Lost Word, Masons strive to uncover the hidden truths within themselves and unlock the mysteries of the universe. Pursuing the Lost Word is a timeless quest for enlightenment and wisdom, guiding Masons towards personal transformation and spiritual fulfilment.

The Three Great Lights

The Three Great Lights of Freemasonry consist of the Volume of Sacred Law, the Square, and the Compass. These symbolic tools guide every Mason, emphasizing the importance of moral conduct, truth, and integrity in their lives and interactions with others. The Volume of Sacred Law represents the divine source of wisdom and truth, providing a moral compass for Masons to navigate life's challenges and temptations. The Square symbolizes honesty, fairness, and ethical rectitude, reminding Masons to act with integrity and uphold the principles of justice and equality. Lastly, the Compass signifies boundaries and limitations, urging Masons to maintain self-discipline, temperance, and balance. Together, these Three Great Lights illuminate the path of righteousness and virtue, guiding Masons towards personal growth, moral enlightenment, and spiritual fulfilment. By adhering to the teachings embodied in the Three Great Lights, Masons strive to live a life of honour, integrity, and service to others, embodying the timeless values of Freemasonry and contributing to the betterment of society.

The Working Tools of a Master Mason

The Working Tools of a Master Mason

The tools of a Master Mason are symbols of the virtues that every person should possess. They serve as a guide for living a life of integrity and moral uprightness. The plumb, square, and level represent truth, morality, and equality. The plumb reminds us to walk uprightly in our thoughts and actions, always striving for honesty and integrity. The square teaches us to act fairly and justly, ensuring our conduct aligns with moral principles. The level reminds us to treat all individuals with respect and dignity, recognizing the inherent equality and worth of every person. By embracing these virtues and embodying the lessons of the working tools, a Master Mason can navigate life's challenges with wisdom and grace, upholding the values of Freemasonry and contributing to the betterment of society.

The Hiramic Legend

The Hiramic Legend is a foundational narrative within Freemasonry, symbolizing themes of sacrifice, rebirth, and the search for truth. Central to the legend is the figure of Hiram Abiff, the chief architect of King Solomon's temple. Hiram's role in constructing the temple is crucial, representing the embodiment of wisdom, skill, and integrity in his craft.

The legend takes a dramatic turn when Hiram is met with betrayal and violence, as three fellow craftsmen demand the secrets of a Master Mason. Refusing to compromise his values, Hiram is struck down, symbolizing the sacrifice of one's principles in the face of adversity. This act of martyrdom underscores the importance of upholding moral integrity and fidelity to one's beliefs, even in the most challenging circumstances.

In the aftermath of Hiram's death, the search for the Lost Word commences, reflecting the eternal quest for spiritual enlightenment and wisdom. Through perseverance and dedication, the Master Masons within the Craft seek to recover Hiram's sacred knowledge, symbolizing the journey towards inner illumination and self-realization.

The Hiramic Legend is a timeless allegory for Masonic teachings, emphasizing integrity, resilience, and the pursuit of truth. By reflecting on Hiram's story, Masons are encouraged to embody these principles in their own lives, striving to uphold the noble ideals of the Craft and honour the legacy of Hiram Abiff.

The Geometry of the Universe

The sacred teachings of Freemasonry delve deep into the intricate tapestry of the universe, where symbolic geometry serves as a guiding light towards understanding the cosmic order. Within the Craft, geometric patterns are more than just shapes and angles - they represent divine harmony and spiritual truths that resonate through the ages. From the square's precision to the circle's infinite potential, each geometric symbol carries profound significance in illuminating the path towards enlightenment.

Geometry, as a key element of Masonic symbolism, mirrors the ancient belief that the universe is a grand design governed by mathematical principles. The square, a symbol of morality and righteousness, reminds Masons of the importance of living a virtuous life in accordance with universal laws. Its four equal sides signify balance, stability, and integrity, guiding individuals towards ethical behaviour and harmony with the world around them.

Similarly, the compass, with its ability to draw perfect circles, represents the infinite and eternal nature of the universe. Just as the compass creates a boundary between the known and the unknown, Masons are encouraged to seek knowledge and explore the mysteries of existence. The circle also embodies unity and completeness, reminding initiates of the interconnectedness of all life and the cyclical nature of reality.

The significance of geometry in Freemasonry goes beyond mere shapes; it embodies the fundamental truths of existence and the interconnectedness of all things. By contemplating the geometric symbolism within the Craft, Masons are encouraged to seek a deeper understanding of themselves and their place in the universe. Through the study of sacred geometry, initiates embark on a journey of self-discovery and enlightenment, unlocking the mysteries of the cosmos and aligning themselves with the divine order of creation.

The Path of Enlightenment
The Path of Enlightenment

In the journey of Freemasonry, the path of enlightenment is a profound and transformative experience. It is a sacred journey that each Mason undertakes, a journey of self-discovery, moral growth, and spiritual awakening.

As Mason progresses along this path, he is guided by the timeless principles and teachings of the Craft. Through ritual, symbolism, and contemplation, he is encouraged to explore the depths of his own being, to confront his weaknesses and limitations, and to strive towards a higher state of consciousness.

The path to enlightenment is not an easy one. It requires dedication, self-discipline, and a willingness to confront the shadows within oneself. It is a journey of self-transformation, where the Mason is called to purify his heart, sharpen his mind, and cultivate his soul.

Along this path, Mason learns to cultivate virtues such as charity, compassion, integrity, and wisdom. He strives to embody the noble ideals of Freemasonry in his daily life, to live in harmony with his fellow beings, and to seek the greater good of humanity.

The path of enlightenment is also a journey of inner alchemy, where Mason works to transmute his base impulses and ego-driven desires into higher spiritual qualities. Through contemplation, meditation, and self-examination, he seeks to awaken the divine spark within himself and align his will with the will of the Great Architect of the Universe.

Ultimately, the path of enlightenment in Freemasonry is a quest for truth, wisdom, and unity. It is a journey towards the light of knowledge and understanding. This journey leads Mason towards his inner sanctum, where he discovers the true nature of his existence and the interconnectedness of all things.

As Mason walks this sacred path, he is reminded that the true secrets of Freemasonry are not hidden in some external repository but within his heart and soul. The path of enlightenment is a journey of discovery, a quest for self-realization, and a transformational process that leads the Mason to the heart of the mysteries of life and existence.

The Inner Work of the Mason
The Inner Work of the Mason

Freemasonry is a journey of self-discovery and inner transformation. As Masons progress through the degrees, they are encouraged to delve deep into their own nature, confronting their flaws and striving towards moral and spiritual perfection. This inner work requires dedication, introspection, and a commitment to personal growth.

Central to the inner work of the Mason is the cultivation of moral virtues such as temperance, fortitude, prudence, and justice. Through reflection on these virtues and their application in daily life, Masons seeks to become better individuals and contribute positively to society. Maintaining moral excellence is a cornerstone of Masonic teachings, guiding members toward self-improvement.

Self-awareness and self-discipline are essential aspects of the inner work undertaken by Masons. By examining their actions, thoughts, and motives with honesty and humility, Masons strive to align themselves with the principles of Freemasonry and uphold its values in all aspects of their lives. This process of self-examination and self-regulation is a lifelong endeavour, requiring a commitment to continual growth and self-improvement.

Another crucial aspect of the inner work of the Mason is the practice of charity and benevolence. By extending a helping hand to those in need and engaging in acts of kindness and compassion, Masons seeks to embody the principles of brotherly love and relief. Through service to others, Masons cultivate a sense of unity and fellowship, recognizing the interconnectedness of all humanity.

Ultimately, the inner work of the Mason is a journey towards enlightenment and self-realization. By embracing the teachings and symbolism of Freemasonry and incorporating them into their daily lives, Masons aspire to reach a higher state of consciousness and understanding. This journey is not one of perfection but of progress, as Masons continually strive to elevate themselves spiritually, intellectually, and morally. The inner work of the Mason is a profound and transformative experience, leading to a deeper understanding of oneself and the world around them.

Conclusion: Unlocking the Mysteries

Throughout this journey into the mysteries of Freemasonry, we have plumbed the depths of esoteric knowledge and explored the inner workings of the Masonic tradition. As we have delved into inner alchemy and self-transformation, we have uncovered profound teachings that can illuminate the path towards spiritual enlightenment.

The inner work of the Mason is a journey of self-discovery and self-improvement. It is a process of peeling back the layers of ego and delusion to reveal the true essence. Through reflection, contemplation, and diligent practice of the Masonic virtues, the individual Mason embarks on a transformative journey towards inner illumination and wisdom.

By unlocking the mysteries of Freemasonry, we open ourselves to a deeper understanding of the world around us and our place within it. The teachings and symbols of the Craft serve as guideposts on the path towards moral and spiritual growth, inspiring us to strive for excellence in all aspects of our lives.

As we conclude our exploration of the secret teachings of Freemasonry, let us carry with us the knowledge that true wisdom is not found in acquiring material wealth or external accolades but in cultivating inner virtue and the pursuit of truth. May we continue to seek light in the darkness, uphold the principles of brotherly love, relief, and truth, and embody the ancient Craft's timeless wisdom in our daily lives.

CHAPTER 9

Freemasonry and the Enlightenment Era

Introduction to the Enlightenment Era

The Enlightenment Era, also known as the Age of Enlightenment, was a profound intellectual and philosophical transformation sweeping Europe in the 18th century. It was a time characterized by a fervent pursuit of knowledge, reason, and individual liberty, challenging established traditions and dogmas. The Enlightenment thinkers, known as philosophes, championed principles such as rationality, empiricism, and scepticism, advocating for using reason and critical thinking in all aspects of life.

This era saw significant advancements in various fields, including science, politics, and philosophy. The Scientific Revolution of the 17th century laid the foundation for the Enlightenment's emphasis on empirical inquiry and scientific progress. Philosophers such as Isaac Newton, John Locke, and Voltaire promoted the idea that human reason could unlock the universe's secrets and improve society.

The Enlightenment also marked an increasing secularism and scepticism towards traditional religious institutions. Philosophers like Denis Diderot and Baron d'Holbach challenged religious authority and advocated for religious tolerance and freedom of thought. This intellectual movement paved the way for separating church and state and promoting individual rights and freedoms.

The Enlightenment Era was marked by a spirit of intellectual curiosity and a belief in the power of human reason to bring about progress and social change. It was a time of revolutionary ideas and transformative thinking that continues to influence our modern world.

Historical Context of Freemasonry in the Enlightenment Era

The Enlightenment Era was a period of intellectual and cultural growth that swept Europe in the 17th and 18th centuries, challenging traditional authority and promoting the ideals of reason, science, and individual liberty. This era saw the rise of critical thinking and the questioning of long-held beliefs, paving the way for significant social and political change.

During this time, Freemasonry emerged as a prominent institution, attracting individuals who valued intellectual exploration and the pursuit of knowledge. Freemasonry provided a platform for like-minded individuals to unite, transcending social and religious barriers to engage in meaningful dialogue and debate.

The values of Freemasonry, such as tolerance, equality, and fraternity, resonated deeply with the ideals of the Enlightenment. Freemasonry promoted the importance of education, reason, and ethical behaviour, aligning closely with the intellectual principles of the era.

As Freemasonry gained popularity across Europe, it became a beacon of enlightenment thought, attracting thinkers, scientists, and political leaders who shared a commitment to progress and social reform. The Masonic lodges served as centres of discussion and exchange, fostering a spirit of camaraderie and collaboration among members.

Freemasonry's historical context in the Enlightenment reflects a time of profound transformation and intellectual ferment. Freemasonry's emphasis on reason, tolerance, and solidarity made it a powerful force for change, shaping the intellectual landscape of the era and leaving a lasting impact on the development of modern society.

The Spread of Freemasonry Across Europe

During the Enlightenment era, Freemasonry experienced a significant spread across Europe. The ideals of the Enlightenment, with its emphasis on reason, progress, and tolerance, resonated with the principles of Freemasonry. As a result, Freemasonry thrived in many European countries, becoming a prominent force in society.

Freemasonry's spread across Europe was facilitated by the social networks formed by its members. Freemasons from different regions often travelled and established connections with each other, leading to the establishment of lodges in various countries. These lodges served as centres of intellectual exchange, where members could discuss and promote Enlightenment ideals.

One key factor in the spread of Freemasonry across Europe was the support it received from influential figures in society. Nobles, intellectuals, and even some monarchs became interested in Freemasonry and joined the fraternity. Their patronage helped to legitimize Freemasonry in the eyes of the public and attract new members from different social strata.

Freemasonry expanded across Europe and adapted to each country's cultural and political context. While the core principles of Freemasonry remained the same, lodges in different countries developed unique rituals and traditions. This flexibility allowed Freemasonry to appeal to a diverse range of individuals and foster a sense of unity among members from various backgrounds.

The spread of Freemasonry across Europe also led to international connections among lodges. Freemasons from different countries exchanged ideas and experiences, contributing to a sense of global fraternity. This international network laid the foundation for the future dissemination of Freemasonry to other parts of the world.

The spread of Freemasonry across Europe during the Enlightenment era was a testament to the fraternity's ability to adapt to changing social and intellectual currents. By embracing the ideals of the Enlightenment and fostering connections across borders, Freemasonry became a powerful force for promoting unity, tolerance, and scholarly exchange in Europe and beyond.

The Influence of Enlightenment Thinkers on Freemasonry

During the Enlightenment, prominent thinkers such as Voltaire, Rousseau, and Montesquieu played significant roles in shaping the values and philosophy of Freemasonry. These philosophers were proponents of reason, science, and individual liberty, ideals that aligned closely with the principles of Freemasonry. Their influence on Freemasonry was profound, as they emphasized the importance of tolerance, virtue, and the pursuit of knowledge.

Voltaire, known for advocating freedom of speech and religious tolerance, reflected these values in his writings and public discourse. His ideas resonated with Freemasons, who sought to create a more enlightened and tolerant society. On the other hand, Rousseau emphasized the importance of social contract and the innate goodness of humanity. His emphasis on the importance of community and social harmony echoed the values of brotherhood and unity that Freemasonry promoted.

Montesquieu, known for his theory of separation of powers, also significantly impacted Freemasonry. His ideas on the need for checks and balances in governance resonated with Freemasons, who believed in balance and harmony in all aspects of life. These Enlightenment thinkers shaped the intellectual landscape of Freemasonry, influencing its teachings and values.

Freemasonry spread across Europe during the Enlightenment and served as a platform for intellectual exchange and debate. Freemasons engaged in discussions on philosophy, politics, science, and ethics, drawing inspiration from the ideas of Enlightenment thinkers. The lodges provided a space for freethinking individuals to unite, share ideas, and challenge traditional beliefs.

The influence of Enlightenment thinkers on Freemasonry was reciprocal, with Freemasonry incorporating many of the values and principles advocated by these philosophers. The commitment to reason, tolerance, and the pursuit of knowledge that characterized the Enlightenment era became central tenets of Freemasonry, shaping its rituals, teachings, and ethics. As a result, Freemasonry became not only a fraternity but also a bastion of Enlightenment ideals, fostering intellectual exchange and promoting social progress.

Freemasonry as a Platform for Intellectual Exchange

During the Enlightenment, Freemasonry emerged as a notable platform for intellectual exchange among individuals seeking to engage in thought-provoking discussions and sharing of ideas. Freemasonry provided a unique space where individuals from diverse backgrounds could discuss philosophy, science, politics, and ethics.

Freemasons' lodge meetings and gatherings were conducive to exchanging knowledge and ideas. Members of the fraternity engaged in lively debates and discussions, drawing inspiration from the intellectual currents of the Enlightenment period. This intellectual exchange helped to foster a culture of critical thinking and open-mindedness among Freemasons.

Freemasonry acted as a melting pot of ideas, attracting men of different professions and beliefs united by their commitment to moral and intellectual improvement. Through their interactions within the lodge, Freemasons had the opportunity to broaden their perspectives, challenge their preconceived notions, and expand their intellectual horizons.

The intellectual exchange within Freemasonry also extended beyond the walls of the lodge. Freemasons were known for engaging with the broader society, promoting Enlightenment ideals such as reason, tolerance, and progress. Freemasons played a significant role in shaping the intellectual landscape of their time through their writings, speeches, and actions.

Freemasonry served as a dynamic forum where individuals could engage in meaningful intellectual discourse, exchange ideas, and contribute to advancing knowledge and understanding. This platform for intellectual exchange enriched the minds of individual Freemasons and had a broader impact on the philosophical currents of the Enlightenment era.

The Impact of Enlightenment Ideas on Masonic Philosophy.
The impact of Enlightenment ideas on Masonic philosophy can be seen in Freemasonry's core principles and values during this era. As Enlightenment thinkers promoted reason, logic, and individual freedom, these ideals found resonance within the Masonic community. Freemasonry, with its emphasis on personal growth, moral virtue, and the pursuit of knowledge, aligned closely with the ideals of the Enlightenment.

One key aspect of this impact was the emphasis on rational inquiry and critical thinking within Masonic teachings. As Freemasonry sought to enlighten its members through symbolic rituals and moral lessons, the influence of Enlightenment philosophy encouraged Masons to question dogma, explore new ideas, and seek knowledge beyond the boundaries of traditional beliefs.

Moreover, the Enlightenment emphasis on equality and human rights also influenced Masonic philosophy during this period. Freemasonry, with its focus on brotherhood and unity among its members, embraced the idea of treating all individuals with respect and dignity, regardless of their background or social status. This commitment to equality mirrored the Enlightenment belief in every individual's inherent worth and potential.

Additionally, the Enlightenment's emphasis on tolerance and religious freedom profoundly impacted Masonic philosophy. As Freemasonry transcended religious and cultural boundaries, it provided a platform for individuals of diverse backgrounds to unite in harmony and mutual respect. The principles of religious tolerance and freedom of conscience advocated by Enlightenment thinkers found expression within Masonic lodges, where members were encouraged to uphold these values in their interactions with one another and the world.

Overall, the impact of Enlightenment ideas on Masonic philosophy during this era was significant and enduring. As Freemasonry embraced the values of reason, liberty, and fraternity, it evolved into a vibrant intellectual and philosophical community that reflected the ideals of the Enlightenment. The fusion of Enlightenment principles with Masonic teachings helped shape Freemasonry's moral, intellectual, and spiritual outlook during this transformative historical period.

Freemasonry's Role in Promoting Religious Tolerance.

During the Enlightenment, Freemasonry was crucial in promoting religious tolerance. As a secret society that welcomed members from different religious backgrounds, Freemasonry provided a platform for individuals to unite in fellowship and harmony, regardless of their religious beliefs. This emphasis on inclusivity and accepting diverse perspectives helped foster mutual respect and understanding among members.

Freemasonry's commitment to religious tolerance was reflected in its rituals and teachings, emphasising the importance of moral values, personal integrity, and the pursuit of truth. Masonic lodges became spaces where individuals could engage in open dialogue and exchange ideas without fear of religious persecution or discrimination. This environment of intellectual freedom and respect for religious diversity starkly contrasted the religious conflicts and intolerance that had plagued Europe for centuries.

By promoting religious tolerance within its ranks, Freemasonry served as a model for a more enlightened and inclusive society.

Members were encouraged to see beyond religious differences and focus on their shared humanity and common values. This spirit of tolerance and acceptance extended beyond the lodge's walls, influencing members to advocate for religious freedom and civil liberties in the broader society.

The embrace of religious tolerance within Freemasonry also profoundly impacted individual members, inspiring them to cultivate a more tolerant and compassionate attitude towards others. This shift in mindset helped to break down barriers of prejudice and foster a sense of unity among people with diverse backgrounds and beliefs. As Freemasons practised the principles of tolerance and understanding within their lodges, they became ambassadors for these ideals in the world at large, promoting a culture of respect and acceptance in their communities.

Freemasonry's commitment to promoting religious tolerance during the Enlightenment Era exemplified its dedication to fostering a more enlightened and harmonious society. By providing a forum for individuals to embrace diversity, engage in meaningful dialogue, and cultivate mutual respect, Freemasonry demonstrated the transformative power of tolerance in creating a more inclusive and harmonious world.

The Connection Between Freemasonry and the Scientific Revolution.

During the Enlightenment, Freemasonry played a significant role in fostering the principles of the Scientific Revolution. Many Enlightenment thinkers who were also Freemasons were proponents of empirical observation, experimentation, and rational inquiry. Freemasonry provided a platform for intellectuals to exchange ideas and knowledge, including scientific advancements.

The connection between Freemasonry and the Scientific Revolution can be seen in the emphasis on critical thinking, open-mindedness, and a quest for knowledge within Masonic lodges. Freemasonry encouraged its members to seek truth and understanding through objective investigation, much like the scientific method advocated by prominent scientists of the time.

The principles of the Scientific Revolution, such as the importance of reason, evidence-based inquiry, and scepticism towards dogma, resonated with the core values of Freemasonry. This alignment led many Enlightenment-era thinkers to embrace scientific advancement and Masonic principles, viewing them as complementary paths towards enlightenment and progress.

In Masonic lodges, discussions on natural philosophy, astronomy, mathematics, and other scientific disciplines were common. Members were encouraged to engage in intellectual debates and share their insights on the natural world. This intellectual exchange helped foster a culture of curiosity and exploration that was characteristic of both the Scientific Revolution and Freemasonry.

Overall, the connection between Freemasonry and the Scientific Revolution during the Enlightenment Era exemplifies the shared values of rationality, inquiry, and the pursuit of knowledge. Freemasonry provided a space for thinkers to engage in scientific discussions and promote the spirit of intellectual curiosity that defined the era's scientific advancements.

Criticisms and Controversies Surrounding Freemasonry in the Enlightenment Era.

One of the primary criticisms levelled against Freemasonry during the Enlightenment Era was its secretive nature. Detractors argued that the clandestine rituals and ceremonies conducted by Masonic lodges were a cause for suspicion and fear. The notion of an exclusive society with its own rituals and symbols raised concerns about potential subversive activities or hidden agendas.

Another criticism aimed at Freemasonry was its perceived challenge to established religious institutions. The emphasis on reason, enlightenment, and tolerance within Masonic teachings contradicted the orthodox beliefs of the Catholic Church and other religious authorities of the time. This conflict led to accusations of heresy and blasphemy against Freemasons, further fuelling the scepticism and criticism surrounding the organization.

Furthermore, Freemasonry's commitment to secularism and the separation of church and state was seen as a threat by those who held power in religious and political spheres. The idea of a society that promoted individual freedoms, democracy, and the pursuit of knowledge outside the control of traditional institutions was met with resistance and condemnation.

Freemasonry's secretive and exclusive nature also led to accusations of elitism and favouritism. Critics argued that Masonic lodges' closed-door meetings and recruitment processes promoted a culture of privilege and nepotism, where influence and advancement were based on connections rather than merit.

Despite these criticisms and controversies, Freemasonry continued to thrive during the Enlightenment Era, attracting diverse intellectuals, scientists, and political figures drawn to its liberty, equality, and fraternity principles. The legacy of Freemasonry in shaping the thought of this period cannot be denied, as it played a significant role in promoting critical thinking, tolerance, and enlightenment ideals that continue to influence society today.

Legacy of Freemasonry in Shaping the Thought of the Enlightenment Period.

During the Enlightenment period, Freemasonry played a significant role in shaping the intellectual landscape of the era. The values of rationality, tolerance, and the pursuit of knowledge were central to Enlightenment thinkers and Freemasonry. Freemasonry provided a space for individuals of diverse backgrounds to come together and engage in philosophical discussions, promoting the exchange of ideas and the spread of knowledge.

One of the critical legacies of Freemasonry in the Enlightenment period was its emphasis on individual liberty and equality. Freemasonry's principles of brotherhood and fellowship transcended social hierarchies, emphasizing each individual's inherent worth and dignity. This promotion of universal equality and freedom values resonated with the Enlightenment thinkers' ideals, who sought to challenge oppressive systems and promote human rights.

Furthermore, Freemasonry's commitment to pursuing knowledge and truth aligned with the Enlightenment thinkers' emphasis on reason and empirical inquiry. Freemasonry's rituals and symbolism were steeped in philosophical and symbolic meaning, encouraging members to seek deeper understanding and contemplation. This emphasis on intellectual curiosity and enlightenment mirrored the Enlightenment thinkers' commitment to advancing knowledge and challenging dogma.

In addition, Freemasonry's promotion of religious tolerance and inclusivity reflected the Enlightenment thinkers' call for religious freedom and pluralism. Freemasonry provided a space where individuals from different religious backgrounds could unite in mutual respect and understanding, fostering a spirit of religious harmony and cooperation. This commitment to religious tolerance was a cornerstone of Freemasonry's influence on the Enlightenment period, contributing to the broader movement towards religious freedom and secularism.

Overall, the legacy of Freemasonry in shaping the thought of the Enlightenment period is evident in its promotion of universal values, intellectual inquiry, religious tolerance, and the pursuit of individual liberty. Freemasonry's influence extended beyond its rituals and traditions, impacting the intellectual and philosophical discourse of the era and contributing to the advancement of Enlightenment ideals.

CHAPTER 10

Freemasonry in the Modern World

Historical Context: Brief overview of Freemasonry's evolution from the Enlightenment era to the present day.
Freemasonry emerged during the Enlightenment era in the early 18th century, drawing inspiration from the intellectual and philosophical developments of the time. While the precise origins of the fraternity remain shrouded in mystery, it is clear that Freemasonry quickly gained traction and evolved into a prominent social and spiritual institution.
Initially rooted in the traditions of medieval stonemasons, Freemasonry gradually transformed into a fraternity that transcended occupational boundaries. During the Enlightenment, Freemasonry attracted individuals from various social classes drawn to its principles of moral virtue, brotherly love, and intellectual curiosity.
As Freemasonry spread across continents, it adapted to the cultural contexts of different countries, incorporating local traditions and beliefs into its rituals and teachings. The fraternity's global influence expanded, establishing lodges in diverse regions and fostering connections between individuals from disparate backgrounds.
In the modern era, Freemasonry faces challenges stemming from shifting societal norms and changing demographics. Membership numbers have fluctuated, leading to efforts to revitalize the organization and attract new generations of members. Despite these challenges, Freemasonry continues to uphold its core values of charity, integrity, and personal growth.
Freemasonry remains a symbol of tradition and camaraderie, offering a space for individuals to connect, reflect, and contribute to their communities. Its historical evolution from the Enlightenment to the present reflects a rich tapestry of shared experiences and enduring principles that continue to shape the fraternity's identity and purpose in the contemporary world.
Global Influence: Exploration of Freemasonry's presence and impact in various countries and cultures worldwide.

Freemasonry's influence is far-reaching and extends beyond geographical boundaries. With a presence in various countries and cultures around the world, the principles and teachings of Freemasonry have left a lasting impact on society. In Europe, Freemasonry has roots dating back to the Enlightenment era, significantly shaping philosophical and political discourse. In the United States, Freemasonry has been intertwined with the country's history, with many influential figures being fraternity members.

In Asia, Freemasonry has adapted to local customs and traditions, fostering a sense of brotherhood among members. Freemasonry has played a role in social activism and community development in Africa. In Latin America, Freemasonry has been a force for social change and has promoted unity among diverse populations. The influence of Freemasonry is not limited to the West but has also spread to the Middle East. Despite challenges and misconceptions, Freemasonry has found a place in Middle Eastern societies, promoting values of tolerance, brotherhood, and mutual respect. Freemasonry has a strong presence in Australia and Oceania, contributing to charitable initiatives and community welfare.

Freemasonry's global influence is a testament to its enduring appeal and relevance in today's interconnected world. By adapting to local cultures and fostering a sense of unity and fellowship, Freemasonry continues to positively impact individuals and communities worldwide.

Challenges and Controversies: Examining the challenges faced by Freemasonry in the modern era, including public perception, membership decline, and external criticism.

In the modern era, Freemasonry has encountered various challenges and controversies that have impacted its reputation and membership numbers. One significant challenge is the public perception of Freemasonry, often tainted by misconceptions and conspiracy theories. Some view Freemasonry as a secretive and exclusive organization, leading to suspicion and distrust from those outside the fraternity.

Furthermore, Freemasonry has faced a decline in membership in recent years, a trend observed across many fraternal organizations. Factors contributing to this decline include shifting societal values, busier lifestyles, and traditional fraternal organisations' perceived lack of relevance in the digital age. As a result, Freemasonry must adapt and evolve to attract and retain new members while honouring its historical traditions and values. External criticism of Freemasonry has also presented challenges in the modern era. Critics raise concerns about the influence of Freemasonry in politics, business, and other institutions, often speculating about hidden agendas and nefarious intentions. Additionally, accusations of elitism and exclusivity have further fuelled negative perceptions of the fraternity.

Despite these challenges, Freemasonry continues to navigate the complexities of the modern world, striving to uphold its core principles of brotherhood, morality, and charity. By addressing these challenges with transparency, engagement, and a commitment to positive change, Freemasonry can overcome obstacles and play a vital role in society. Social and Community Engagement: Discussion of Freemasonry's involvement in charitable endeavours, community outreach, and philanthropic efforts.

Freemasonry has a long-standing tradition of engaging in charitable endeavours, community outreach, and philanthropic efforts. Across the globe, Masonic organizations have been actively involved in various initiatives to support those in need and positively impact society. Freemasonry's commitment to social and community engagement is a cornerstone of its ethos, from fundraising for local community projects to supporting healthcare initiatives and educational programs.

One of the critical aspects of Freemasonry's social engagement is its focus on charitable giving. Masonic lodges often organize fundraising events and activities to raise money for charitable causes, such as financial assistance to individuals facing hardship, supporting local organizations and charities, and contributing to disaster relief efforts. Through these initiatives, Freemasonry demonstrates its commitment to helping those less fortunate and making a difference in the lives of others.

In addition to charitable giving, Freemasonry also actively engages in community outreach programs. Masonic lodges frequently collaborate with local community groups, schools, and organizations to support community development projects, educational initiatives, and cultural events. By fostering strong relationships with the communities in which they operate, Masonic organizations aim to promote unity, understanding, and positive social change.

Moreover, Freemasonry's philanthropic efforts extend beyond individual communities to encompass larger-scale projects and programs. Many Masonic organizations run national or international charitable campaigns focused on specific causes, such as healthcare research, youth education, and environmental conservation. Through these broader initiatives, Freemasonry seeks to address pressing social issues and contribute to the greater good of society.

Freemasonry's dedication to social and community engagement underscores its commitment to serving humanity and promoting positive values. By actively participating in charitable endeavours, community outreach, and philanthropic efforts, Masonic organizations demonstrate their ongoing commitment to making a meaningful impact on the world around them. Gender Equality: Analysis of the changing attitudes towards gender in Freemasonry, including the rise of co-ed and women-only Masonic organizations.

Freemasonry has traditionally been a male-dominated organization with a long history of excluding women from its ranks. However, in recent years, there has been a significant shift in attitudes towards gender within Freemasonry. This shift has led to the rise of co-ed and women-only Masonic organizations, challenging the traditional gender norms within the fraternity.

Including women in Freemasonry has been a topic of much debate and controversy. Some argue that allowing women to join would detract from the historical and symbolic significance of the all-male brotherhood. However, others believe it is essential to modernize and adapt to changing societal norms to remain relevant and inclusive.

Co-ed Masonic organizations, where both men and women can become members, have emerged as a response to calls for greater gender equality within Freemasonry. These organizations seek to create a more inclusive and diverse environment, breaking down barriers based on gender and fostering a sense of unity among all individuals interested in the Masonic traditions.

Women-only Masonic organizations have also gained prominence, allowing women to engage in Freemasonry's rituals, teachings, and fellowship in an exclusively female setting. These organizations offer a unique perspective on Masonic principles and practices, allowing women to explore and experience the fraternity in their own way.

The rise of co-ed and women-only Masonic organizations reflects a broader trend towards inclusivity and diversity within Freemasonry. As the fraternity continues to evolve and adapt to the changing world, accepting women as equal members is a significant step towards creating a more equitable and welcoming Masonic community for all.

Technology and Communication: Exploration of how modern technology has influenced the practices and communication within Freemasonry, including online resources and virtual meetings.

Modern technology has significantly impacted the practices and communication within Freemasonry, ushering in a new era of connectivity and accessibility for members worldwide. Online resources have revolutionized how Freemasons access information, engage with educational materials and stay connected with their lodges and brethren. Virtual meetings have become increasingly popular, providing opportunities for members to participate in discussions, ceremonies, and lectures from the comfort of their homes.

Digital communication channels, such as email, social media platforms, and dedicated online forums, have facilitated faster and more efficient exchange of ideas and information among Freemasons. These tools have also been instrumental in promoting collaboration and fostering a sense of unity within the global Masonic community. Online libraries and archives have made it easier for members to delve into Masonic history, symbolism, and teachings, enriching their understanding and appreciation of the craft.

Moreover, technological advancements have enabled lodges to conduct virtual degree work, initiation ceremonies, and mentorship programs, ensuring that the traditions and knowledge of Freemasonry are passed down to new generations of Masons. Virtual platforms have also allowed for greater participation and inclusivity, breaking down geographical barriers and enabling brethren from diverse backgrounds to connect and share their experiences.

As Freemasonry continues to embrace modern technology and digital tools, it is essential to strike a balance between incorporating innovative practices and upholding the timeless traditions and values of the craft. By leveraging the power of technology for communication and education, Freemasonry can adapt to the changing times while remaining true to its brotherly love, relief, and truth principles.

Environmental Sustainability: Consideration of Freemasonry's stance on environmental issues and efforts towards promoting sustainability and conservation.

Freemasonry, an ancient and revered institution, has always strongly emphasised moral values and ethical behaviour. Freemasonry is not immune to environmental sustainability and conservation concerns in the modern era. Recognizing the critical importance of protecting our planet for future generations, Freemasonry has taken proactive steps to address environmental issues and promote sustainability.

Within the Masonic community, there is a growing awareness of the need to adopt eco-friendly practices and reduce our carbon footprint. Many Masonic lodges have implemented measures to minimize waste, conserve energy, and promote recycling. By embracing sustainable initiatives, Freemasonry aims to set an example for its members and the broader community on the importance of environmental stewardship.

Furthermore, Freemasonry's commitment to environmental sustainability extends beyond its own practices. Many Masonic organizations actively support environmental causes and partner with conservation groups to protect the natural world. Freemasons demonstrate their dedication to preserving the planet and combating climate change by participating in tree-planting initiatives, beach clean-ups, and conservation projects.

One of the core principles of Freemasonry is the idea of leaving a positive legacy for future generations. By promoting environmental sustainability and conservation, Freemasonry upholds this principle and recognizes the interconnectedness of all living beings. Through their actions and advocacy, Freemasons seek to inspire others to join in the effort to safeguard the environment and create a more sustainable world for all.

In conclusion, Freemasonry's stance on environmental issues reflects its core values of morality, responsibility, and stewardship. By embracing sustainability and conservation practices, Freemasonry demonstrates its commitment to creating a better future for all and leaving a lasting legacy of environmental awareness and action. Diversity and Inclusion: Examination of efforts to diversify and broaden the membership base of Freemasonry, promoting inclusivity and unity among all individuals

Freemasonry is an ancient and esteemed institution that has long been associated with tradition, secrecy, and exclusivity. However, in recent years, there has been a notable shift towards promoting diversity and inclusion within the ranks of Freemasonry. Recognizing the importance of embracing individuals from all backgrounds, Freemasonry has made concerted efforts to broaden its membership base and foster a culture of inclusivity and unity.

One of the critical principles of Freemasonry is that all individuals are equal regardless of their background, social status, or beliefs. This core tenet has increased the emphasis on diversity within the organization, encouraging individuals from diverse backgrounds to join and participate in its rituals and teachings. By actively reaching out to individuals from different cultures, ethnicities, and socio-economic backgrounds, Freemasonry is working towards creating a more representative and inclusive community.

Many Masonic lodges have implemented initiatives to promote diversity and inclusion to attract a more diverse membership base. This includes outreach programs targeted towards underrepresented communities, scholarships for individuals who may not have the financial means to join, and educational campaigns to dispel misconceptions and myths surrounding Freemasonry. By providing opportunities for individuals from all walks of life to become a part of the Masonic Brotherhood, Freemasonry strives to create a more inclusive and welcoming environment for all.

Furthermore, Freemasonry is committed to fostering a sense of unity among its members, regardless of their differences. Through shared rituals, teachings, and values, Freemasonry seeks to create a sense of camaraderie and brotherhood that transcends individual differences. By promoting mutual respect, understanding, and acceptance, Freemasonry aims to build a community that embraces diversity and celebrates the unique contributions of each member.

In conclusion, efforts to diversify and broaden the membership base of Freemasonry are essential to ensure the continued relevance and vibrancy of the institution in the modern world. By promoting inclusivity, unity, and respect for all individuals, Freemasonry is laying the foundation for a more diverse and harmonious community that reflects the values of equality and brotherhood at its core.

 Education and Research: Highlighting the importance of education and research within Freemasonry, including the preservation of Masonic history and teachings

Education and research play a vital role within Freemasonry, serving as pillars that uphold the rich history and teachings of the organization. Through a commitment to lifelong learning and intellectual curiosity, Freemasons can deepen their understanding of the craft, enhance their personal development, and contribute to preserving Masonic traditions for future generations.

Masonic education encompasses various topics, from symbols and rituals to moral philosophy and esoteric teachings. By engaging in educational activities such as lectures, discussions, study groups, and workshops, members can deepen their knowledge and strengthen their connection to the principles and values espoused by Freemasonry. This continued pursuit of knowledge enriches the individual Mason's experience. It fosters a sense of camaraderie and shared learning within the Masonic community.

Research also plays a crucial role in preserving and disseminating Masonic history and teachings. Scholars and enthusiasts within the fraternity dedicate themselves to uncovering hidden insights, exploring historical documents, and unravelling the mysteries at Freemasonry's heart. By conducting rigorous research and documentation, Masonic scholars help illuminate the origins and evolution of the craft, shedding light on its profound symbolism, traditions, and practices.

The importance of education and research within Freemasonry extends beyond the individual member to the broader Masonic community. By encouraging a culture of learning and intellectual inquiry, Freemasonry can evolve and adapt to the ever-changing needs and challenges of the modern world. Through scholarly pursuits and knowledge sharing, Freemasons can work together to ensure the continuity and relevance of Masonic teachings for generations to come. In this way, education and research serve as vital tools in preserving and enriching Freemasonry's timeless legacy.

Future Prospects: Speculation on Freemasonry's future direction and relevance in the ever-evolving modern world, considering potential challenges and opportunities for growth and adaptation.

As we look ahead to the future of Freemasonry in the modern world, it is essential to consider the potential challenges and opportunities. One of Freemasonry's key challenges is the decline in membership in many parts of the world. Freemasonry must adapt to attract and retain new members who resonate with its principles and values to ensure its continued relevance and sustainability.

Freemasonry must also leverage technology to enhance its communication and outreach efforts in an increasingly digital and interconnected society. Embracing online platforms for education, networking, and collaboration can help broaden Freemasonry's reach and engage with a broader audience.

Furthermore, Freemasonry has the opportunity to strengthen its impact on society by focusing on social and environmental issues. By actively participating in charitable endeavours, promoting environmental sustainability, and advocating for positive change, Freemasonry can demonstrate its commitment to making a difference in the world.

Fostering diversity and inclusivity within Freemasonry is crucial for its growth and relevance in the modern era. Embracing individuals from diverse backgrounds and perspectives can enrich the Masonic experience and strengthen the bonds of brotherhood among members.

As Freemasonry navigates future challenges, it is essential to remain dedicated to its core principles and be willing to adapt and evolve. By staying true to its values and embracing change, Freemasonry can continue to thrive and make a meaningful impact in the ever-evolving modern world.

CHAPTER 11

The Future of Freemasonry

Introduction to the Changing Landscape of Freemasonry

As Freemasonry continues to evolve in the modern era, the changing landscape presents challenges and opportunities for the organization. The traditions and values upheld by Freemasonry remain steadfast. Still, how they are practised and communicated is constantly being redefined. Freemasonry must adapt to new technologies and innovations in today's fast-paced, interconnected world to stay relevant and attract a diverse membership.

One of the critical aspects of the changing landscape of Freemasonry is the increasing reliance on technology to facilitate communication and organization within lodges. Digital platforms and tools allow members to connect, share information, and coordinate activities more effectively. From online forums and social media channels to virtual meeting platforms, technology has the potential to enhance the way Freemasons interact with one another and engage with the broader community.

Furthermore, embracing innovation in ritual practices and educational programs can breathe new life into Masonic traditions, making them more accessible and engaging for a younger generation of members. Incorporating multimedia elements, interactive workshops, and other modern teaching methods can foster a deeper understanding of Masonic principles and values, ensuring they are passed down effectively to future generations.

By embracing technology and innovation, Freemasonry can adapt to the changing needs and preferences of its membership while also remaining true to its core principles and heritage. As the organization looks to the future, navigating the evolving landscape of Freemasonry will require a willingness to explore new possibilities and embrace change while staying true to the timeless values that have defined the craft for centuries.

Embracing Technology and Innovation in Freemasonry

Technology and innovation have become integral components in the evolution of Freemasonry. As the world advances rapidly,

Freemasonry must also embrace these changes to stay relevant and vibrant in today's society. One critical way Freemasonry can harness technology's power is through online platforms and digital tools. These tools can streamline communication among members, provide educational resources, and facilitate organising events and activities. Virtual meetings and webinars can also be utilized to connect members worldwide, fostering a sense of unity and collaboration. By leveraging technology, Freemasonry can adapt to the digital age while maintaining its core values and traditions.

Adapting to Social Changes and Diversity

As Freemasonry continues to evolve in the modern world, it faces the challenge of adapting to social changes and embracing diversity within its membership. In today's society, there is a growing emphasis on inclusivity and equality, prompting Freemasonry to reflect on its traditions and practices to ensure they resonate with a more diverse and socially aware population.

Freemasonry fundamentally adapts to social changes by actively promoting diversity and inclusivity within its ranks. Efforts are being made to reach out to individuals from diverse backgrounds and cultures, welcoming them into the fraternity with open arms. This inclusivity strengthens the Masonic community and aligns with Freemasonry's values of equality and unity.

Moreover, Freemasonry is also addressing social changes by embracing gender equality. While traditionally a male-only organization, many branches of Freemasonry have started to welcome women into their ranks, recognizing the importance of gender diversity in today's society. Many have met This decision enthusiastically, as it signifies a progressive and inclusive approach to membership.

Furthermore, Freemasonry is adapting to social changes by actively engaging with modern issues and concerns. Whether supporting social justice initiatives, promoting ethical business practices, or advocating for environmental sustainability, Freemasonry is committed to positively impacting society. By aligning its values with contemporary social priorities, Freemasonry remains relevant and responsive to the world's changing needs.

In conclusion, adapting to social changes and diversity is crucial for Freemasonry's continued relevance and growth. By embracing inclusivity, gender equality, and engagement with modern issues, Freemasonry reaffirms its commitment to creating a more open, diverse, and socially conscious fraternity.

Sustainable Practices and Environmental Awareness in Freemasonry

Freemasonry has a long tradition of upholding values that promote harmony, balance, and stewardship of the environment. In today's world, as the impact of human activities on the planet becomes increasingly evident, Freemasonry needs to embrace sustainable practices and environmental awareness. By integrating these principles into its teachings and activities, Freemasonry can play a valuable role in fostering a more sustainable and ecologically conscious society.

One key aspect of sustainable practices within Freemasonry is the promotion of energy efficiency and environmental conservation in its buildings and meeting spaces. By adopting green building practices, such as using recycled materials, energy-efficient lighting, and water-saving fixtures, Masonic lodges can reduce their environmental footprint and contribute to a healthier planet.

Furthermore, Freemasonry can raise awareness about environmental issues and encourage its members to take individual action to protect the environment. By organizing community clean-up events, tree-planting initiatives, and educational programs on sustainability, Freemasonry can inspire its members to become environmental stewards in their everyday lives.

In addition to promoting sustainable practices, Freemasonry can integrate environmental awareness into its symbolic teachings and rituals. By incorporating themes of interconnectedness, balance, and respect for nature into its ceremonies, Freemasonry can instil a deeper appreciation for the natural world and the importance of living in harmony with it.

By embracing sustainable practices and environmental awareness, Freemasonry can contribute to a more sustainable planet and reinforce its core values of unity, brotherhood, and service to humanity. Through collective action and a commitment to environmental stewardship, Freemasonry can lead by example and inspire positive change in the world.

Enhancing Community Engagement and Philanthropy

Freemasonry strongly emphasises community engagement and philanthropy, embodying the principles of charity and service to others. Freemasons aim to positively impact society and help those in need through various initiatives and projects. By working together and pooling resources, Freemasons have supported a wide range of charitable causes and contributed to the well-being of their communities.

One of the key ways in which Freemasonry enhances community engagement is through its charitable activities. Freemasons regularly donate to charitable organizations, support local community projects, and assist those facing hardships. By giving back to the community, Freemasons strive to create a more compassionate and inclusive society where everyone can thrive.

In addition to financial contributions, Freemasonry encourages its members to actively engage in volunteer work and community service. By volunteering their time and expertise, Freemasons can directly impact the lives of those in need and help create positive change in their communities. Whether organizing a food drive, participating in a community cleanup project, or volunteering at a local shelter, Freemasons are dedicated to serving others and making a difference.

Furthermore, Freemasonry fosters a spirit of philanthropy among its members, inspiring them to embody the values of generosity, compassion, and selflessness. By promoting a culture of giving and service, Freemasonry benefits the recipients of its charitable efforts and enriches the lives of its members, instilling a sense of fulfilment and purpose.

Through its commitment to community engagement and philanthropy, Freemasonry continues to uphold its tradition of positively impacting society and fostering a spirit of unity and cooperation among its members.

Addressing Challenges and Controversies within Freemasonry

Throughout its long history, Freemasonry has faced challenges and controversies that have tested its core values and principles. One of the most persistent challenges has been the perception of secrecy and exclusivity that surrounds Freemasonry. Critics often raise concerns about the closed nature of Masonic rituals and ceremonies, fuelling speculation and mistrust among the general public.

Another issue that Freemasonry has grappled with is the question of gender inclusivity. Traditionally a male-only organization, Freemasonry has faced criticism for excluding women from its ranks. In recent years, some branches of Freemasonry have begun to embrace gender diversity, welcoming women into their lodges and fostering a more inclusive and egalitarian environment.

Furthermore, Freemasonry has not been immune to controversies surrounding its alleged connections to political power and influence. Conspiracy theories abound, linking Freemasonry to secret societies and shadowy agendas. Addressing these misconceptions and misconstrued beliefs has been an ongoing challenge for the Freemason community.

Freemasonry must be committed to transparency, openness, and inclusivity in response to these challenges and controversies. By fostering dialogue, engaging with the wider community, and promoting ethical values, Freemasonry can overcome these obstacles and continue to thrive in the modern world. Through education, outreach, and a dedication to its founding principles, Freemasonry can navigate the complexities of the contemporary landscape and emerge as a beacon of moral virtue and social responsibility.

Nurturing Leadership and Mentorship Programs

Leadership and mentorship are essential aspects of Freemasonry that play a crucial role in shaping the organisation's future. As Freemasonry continues to evolve in a rapidly changing world, it is vital to cultivate strong leadership skills and establish effective mentorship programs to ensure the continuity and success of the fraternity.

Effective leadership within Freemasonry involves inspiring and guiding members to uphold the values and principles of the organization. Strong leaders lead by example, demonstrating integrity, compassion, and a commitment to the fraternity's goals. Through their guidance and vision, leaders can inspire others to strive for excellence and contribute positively to their communities.

Mentorship programs provide valuable opportunities for experienced Freemasons to pass their knowledge and wisdom to younger members. Mentors serve as role models and advisors, offering guidance and support to help mentees navigate their Masonic journey. Freemasonry can preserve its traditions and values by fostering strong mentorship relationships while empowering the next generation of leaders.

Nurturing leadership and mentorship programs within Freemasonry requires a commitment to ongoing education and development. Leadership training, workshops, and resources can help members enhance their leadership skills and capabilities. Similarly, creating structured mentorship programs that pair experienced Masons with newer members can foster meaningful connections and facilitate knowledge sharing within the fraternity.

By investing in leadership and mentorship initiatives, Freemasonry can cultivate a thriving community of dedicated members who are equipped to lead with integrity and uphold the timeless principles of the organization. Freemasonry can continue to adapt and thrive in a dynamic global landscape through a collective effort to nurture leadership potential and facilitate mentorship relationships.

Global Expansion and Collaboration with Other Organizations

Global Expansion and Collaboration with Other Organizations:

As Freemasonry continues to adapt and evolve in the modern world, there is a growing emphasis on global expansion and collaboration with other organizations. Freemasonry can enhance its reach and impact on a broader scale by forming partnerships and alliances with various groups and institutions.

One of the critical benefits of global expansion and collaboration is the opportunity to exchange ideas and best practices with like-minded organizations. By sharing knowledge and resources,

Freemasonry can strengthen its foundation and create a more inclusive and diverse community. This collaboration also allows for the promotion of mutual values and principles across different cultural contexts.

Furthermore, through strategic partnerships with other organizations, Freemasonry can broaden its philanthropic efforts, and support causes that align with its core values. Freemasonry can amplify its impact and make a greater societal difference by working with other groups.

Global expansion also opens up new opportunities for cultural exchange and learning. By engaging with organizations from around the world, Freemasonry can enrich its traditions and rituals, incorporating diverse perspectives and practices into its fabric.

In an increasingly interconnected world, collaboration with other organizations is essential for Freemasonry to thrive and remain relevant. By embracing this spirit of cooperation and openness, Freemasonry can continue to grow and adapt to the changing landscape of the modern era.

Preserving Traditions while Embracing Modernity

As Freemasonry continues to adapt to the changing world around it, there is an ongoing effort to balance the preservation of traditional values and practices with the need to embrace modernity. This delicate balance ensures that Freemasonry's core principles and rituals remain intact while allowing for growth and relevance in contemporary society.

One of the key ways in which Freemasonry preserves its traditions while embracing modernity is through its focus on symbolism and allegory. Symbols and symbolic teachings date back to the earliest days of Freemasonry. It remains a vital part of the organization today. By maintaining these traditional teaching methods, Freemasonry can effectively communicate its values and lessons to new generations of members.

Another way Freemasonry balances tradition with modernity is by incorporating technology and innovation into its practices.

While Freemasonry's core rituals and ceremonies remain unchanged, the organization has embraced technology to streamline administrative tasks, facilitate communication among members, and reach a wider audience. Using online platforms, virtual meetings, and digital resources has allowed Freemasonry to adapt to the digital age while still upholding its timeless traditions.

In addition, Freemasonry has recognized the importance of diversity and inclusivity in today's world. By welcoming members from all backgrounds and walks of life, Freemasonry ensures its traditions remain relevant and accessible to various individuals. Embracing diversity not only enriches the Masonic experience but also helps the organization stay connected to the diverse communities it serves.

By carefully preserving its traditions while embracing modernity, Freemasonry continues to evolve and thrive in the ever-changing landscape of the 21st century. This balance ensures that Freemasonry's timeless teachings and values remain relevant and impactful for future generations.

Conclusion: The Continued Relevance and Evolution of Freemasonry

Freemasonry's enduring relevance lies in its ability to adapt and evolve while staying true to its core principles and traditions. As society changes and technology advances, Freemasonry must embrace innovation and modernity to remain a vibrant and influential organization.

By preserving its rich history and rituals, Freemasonry can provide a sense of continuity and connection to its members while engaging with the contemporary world. Embracing diversity and inclusivity, Freemasonry can attract new members who bring fresh perspectives and ideas to the organization.

Freemasonry can demonstrate its commitment to social responsibility and ethical leadership through sustainable practices and environmental awareness. By actively engaging with the community and supporting charitable initiatives, Freemasonry can positively impact society and enhance its reputation as a force for good.

As Freemasonry continues to evolve and adapt to the changing landscape of the modern world, it must also preserve its traditions and values that have guided the organization for centuries. By balancing tradition and innovation, Freemasonry can ensure its continued relevance and impact for generations.

CHAPTER 12

The Legacy of Freemasonry

Freemasonry, with its intricate rituals, symbolic teachings, and rich history, has profoundly influenced the fabric of society across continents and epochs. Beyond its outward practices and visible symbols, Freemasonry's enduring legacy is deeply intertwined with the evolution of human consciousness and the quest for self-transformation.

At its core, Freemasonry is a timeless repository of esoteric knowledge and spiritual wisdom, drawing upon ancient teachings and mystical traditions from various cultures and philosophies. Encoded within its rituals and symbols are layers of meaning that speak to the deeper mysteries of existence, inviting initiates to embark on an inner journey of self-discovery and self-realization. Through contemplation and reflection on the symbolic lessons of the Craft, Freemasons are guided towards a deeper understanding of the universal truths that underlie the human experience.

The origin of Freemasonry can be traced back to the cathedral-building guilds of the Middle Ages, where skilled artisans gathered to share knowledge, uphold ethical standards, and foster a sense of kinship. Over time, these operative lodges transitioned into speculative Freemasonry, welcoming men of noble character and moral integrity into their ranks. The fraternity quickly became a sanctuary for seekers of wisdom and truth, offering a sanctuary for like-minded individuals to unite in camaraderie and mutual support.

The symbolic tools of the operative mason – the compass, the square, and the plumb rule – serve as potent metaphors for the moral and spiritual work undertaken within the Masonic lodge. The compass reminds Freemasons to circumscribe their desires and passions within due bounds, maintaining a balance between life's material and spiritual aspects. The square symbolizes the importance of honesty, integrity, and ethical conduct in all dealings, guiding Masons to act uprightly and justly in their interactions with others. The plumb rule serves as a reminder to lead a life of righteousness and moral equilibrium, striving for inner harmony and alignment with divine principles.

Beyond its symbolic language and ceremonial practices, Freemasonry's impact extends into social responsibility and philanthropy. Freemasons worldwide are committed to charitable endeavours, supporting various causes, from healthcare and education to disaster relief and community development. The ethos of brotherly love and mutual aid that underpins Freemasonry inspires members to extend a helping hand to those in need, embodying the values of compassion, generosity, and solidarity.

In the grand tapestry of human history, Freemasonry stands as a beacon of light and guidance, illuminating the path of self-discovery, moral enlightenment, and social responsibility. Freemasonry's timeless teachings and practices offer a transformative experience for those who seek a deeper understanding of themselves and the world around them. The legacy of Freemasonry is a testament to the enduring power of wisdom, fraternity, and service, serving as a source of inspiration and guidance for generations to come.

Freemasonry's influence can also be seen in politics and governance, with many influential figures throughout history being members of the Craft. From world leaders to intellectuals, Freemasonry has attracted individuals seeking to uphold liberty, equality, and fraternity principles. The values espoused within Masonic teachings often resonate with movements advocating for social justice, human rights, and democratic ideals.

The symbolism used in Freemasonry is rich with layers of meaning, drawing upon both ancient symbols and universal archetypes to convey profound truths about the nature of reality and the human experience. Symbols such as the all-seeing eye, the blazing star, and the trowel serve as visual mnemonics that prompt contemplation and reflection on deeper philosophical concepts. These symbols are not meant to be interpreted narrowly but encourage multiple interpretations that speak to the complexity of human existence and spiritual evolution.

Freemasonry's emphasis on moral development and personal growth is manifested through its system of degrees, each offering a new perspective on the Craft and new opportunities for self-improvement. The allegorical dramas enacted within the lodge and the esoteric teachings passed down through generations are tools for inner transformation and spiritual enlightenment. By engaging with these teachings and principles, Freemasons are encouraged to cultivate virtues such as wisdom, temperance, and fortitude, guiding them towards a more harmonious and virtuous way of life.

In conclusion, Freemasonry continues to be a beacon of light and wisdom in a complex and ever-changing world. Its teachings, rituals, and symbolism offer a path towards self-discovery, moral growth, and spiritual evolution for those who seek a deeper understanding of themselves and the universe. The profound legacy of Freemasonry endures as a testament to the enduring power of wisdom, fraternity, and service, inspiring generations to come with its timeless message of unity, brotherly love, and the pursuit of truth.

CHAPTER 13

The Hidden Symbols of Freemasonry

The symbolism embedded within Freemasonry's ancient and revered institution is a profound language that speaks to the hearts and minds of initiates, guiding them on a transformative journey towards self-discovery, moral awakening, and spiritual enlightenment. Each emblem and design within the Masonic tradition holds a depth of meaning and significance that transcends the ordinary realm of understanding, inviting seekers to delve deeper into the mysteries of existence and uncover the hidden truths beneath the surface.

The Square and Compasses, the iconic emblem of Freemasonry, are a powerful reminder of the timeless principles of moral rectitude and self-mastery. With its four sides symbolizing morality, fairness, integrity, and honesty, the Square acts as a beacon calling Masons to uphold these virtues in all their actions and interactions. It serves as a guidepost for ethical conduct and honourable behaviour, urging initiates to abide by the strict measurements of justice and truth in their daily lives. The Square also represents the earthly realm and the material world, reminding Freemasons to ground themselves in reality and uphold moral values in their interactions with others.

The Compasses, with their ability to draw perfect circles and arcs, represent the importance of self-control, balance, and restraint. They challenge Freemasons to rein in their passions and desires, guiding them towards harmonising their inner selves. The Compasses symbolize spiritual boundaries and self-discipline, encouraging initiates to navigate the complexities of life with grace and wisdom. By using the Compasses to circumscribe their desires and align themselves with divine principles, Masons can find inner peace and achieve spiritual equilibrium.

The All-Seeing Eye, encircled by a radiant triangle, gazes down upon Masons as a symbol of divine omniscience and cosmic consciousness. It serves as a constant reminder of the eternal watchfulness of a higher power, urging initiates to align themselves with the will of the Creator and walk the path of truth and wisdom. The All-Seeing Eye offers guidance and protection to those who seek enlightenment, encouraging them to pursue moral excellence, spiritual growth, and ethical conduct in all areas of their lives. The triangle surrounding the All-Seeing Eye represents the Holy Trinity and the interconnectedness of body, mind, and spirit, reminding Freemasons of cultivating harmony and balance within themselves.

The Blazing Star, a symbol of enlightenment and truth, emanates with the divine light of knowledge and understanding, beckoning Freemasons to follow its illuminating path out of the shadows of ignorance and into the brilliance of enlightenment. This radiant symbol represents the eternal quest for spiritual awakening and personal development, inspiring initiates to seek the light of truth amidst a world filled with falsehood and illusion. Through contemplation and meditation on the Blazing Star, Masons can ignite the spark of inner wisdom and ascend to higher levels of consciousness and awareness. The six points of the Blazing Star symbolize the virtues of faith, hope, charity, prudence, fortitude, and temperance, guiding Freemasons towards a life of virtue and integrity.

The Pillars of Boaz and Jachin, standing as ancient sentinels at the threshold of Masonic initiation, embody strength, establishment, and equilibrium. The Pillar of Boaz, signifying strength, grit, and resilience, calls on Masons to stand firm in the face of adversity and challenge, embodying the inner courage and perseverance needed to navigate life's trials gracefully. The Pillar of Jachin, symbolizing establishment, balance, and support, emphasizes cultivating a solid foundation of ethical principles and moral values. It signifies the necessity of finding a harmonious balance between the material and spiritual aspects of existence, fostering a sense of stability, security, and equilibrium in a world filled with uncertainty. The Pillars of Boaz and Jachin remind Freemasons to seek strength and stability within themselves, drawing upon the ancient wisdom of the craft to navigate life's twists and turns with grace and dignity.

In conclusion, the hidden symbols of Freemasonry serve as gateways to deeper understanding, guiding initiates on a sacred journey of self-discovery, moral refinement, and spiritual enlightenment. Through contemplation and introspection on these sacred emblems, Freemasons can unlock the mysteries of existence and unveil the eternal truths at the heart of the human experience and the cosmic order. Embracing the transformative power of symbolism initiates can embark on a profound quest for self-realization, guided by the eternal light of truth and wisdom that shines brightly within the sacred teachings of Freemasonry.

CHAPTER 14

The Hidden Truths of Freemasonry

The enigmatic and ancient institution of Freemasonry continues to captivate the minds of those who seek to unravel its hidden truths and delve into the esoteric mysteries that lie beneath the surface. As one delves deeper into the rich tapestry of symbolism and ritual within Freemasonry, a profound philosophy emerges, offering insights into the nature of existence and the secrets of the universe.

At the heart of Freemasonry's teachings is the profound concept of the "Great Architect of the Universe," a symbolic representation of the divine intelligence that underlies all creation. This divine force is seen as the guiding hand behind the intricate design of the cosmos, weaving together the stars, planets, and all living beings in a harmonious web of interconnectedness. By acknowledging and venerating this higher power, Freemasons seek to align themselves with the cosmic order and draw inspiration from the source of all life.

The symbols used in Freemasonry are not merely superficial emblems but are keys to unlocking deeper truths and spiritual insights. From the square and compass to the blazing star and the pillars of Wisdom, Strength, and Beauty, each symbol carries layers of meaning that resonate with the initiate on a profound level. Through contemplation and reflection on these symbols, Freemasons are guided on a journey of self-discovery and personal transformation, uncovering hidden aspects of themselves and the world around them.

The roots of Freemasonry can be traced back to ancient mystery schools and esoteric traditions that sought to impart wisdom and knowledge of the divine mysteries to those deemed worthy of initiation. Drawing on the symbolism and teachings of these ancient traditions, Freemasonry carries on the lineage of sacred knowledge, preserving and transmitting the ages' esoteric wisdom to those seeking enlightenment.

Central to the practice of Freemasonry is the pursuit of truth, morality, and self-improvement. Through the transformative experience of initiation and participation in the rituals of the craft, members are encouraged to confront their fears, challenge their assumptions, and strive for personal growth and spiritual development. By embodying the virtues of wisdom, strength, and beauty in their daily lives, Freemasons seek to become agents of positive change in the world, upholding the values of brotherly love, relief, and truth in all their actions.

In embracing the hidden truths of Freemasonry, initiates embark on a journey of self-discovery and inner alchemy, seeking to unlock the secrets of the universe and understand their place within the grand design of creation. Through diligent study, reflection, and practice, Freemasons strive to embody the highest ideals of the craft and contribute to the evolution of humanity towards a more enlightened and harmonious future.

The symbolism within Freemasonry is a reflection of the universal truths that bind all of existence together. The square represents the importance of morality, encouraging members to lead a virtuous life. On the other hand, the compass symbolizes the importance of maintaining boundaries and staying within the bounds of moral conduct.

The blazing star, often found in Masonic lodges, symbolises divine guidance and enlightenment. It reminds Freemasons to seek light and knowledge in their journey towards self-improvement and enlightenment. The pillars of Wisdom, Strength, and Beauty signify the well-rounded development of an individual, combining intellectual prowess, inner strength, and an appreciation for aesthetics and harmony.

Freemasonry's emphasis on brotherly love and relief reminds one of the importance of compassion and support for fellow human beings. By embodying these values in their interactions with others, Freemasons aim to create a more harmonious and compassionate society based on mutual respect and understanding.

As Freemasons delve into the rituals and teachings of the craft, they are encouraged to explore the depths of their psyche and confront their innermost fears and desires. By embarking on this journey of self-discovery and self-improvement, initiates can transcend their limitations and strive towards a higher state of consciousness and spiritual understanding. Through this process of inner alchemy, Freemasons seek to unlock their hidden potential and tap into the universal truths that connect all beings in a web of interconnectedness.

In embracing Freemasonry's profound philosophy and symbolism, initiates open themselves to a world of esoteric knowledge and spiritual wisdom that transcends the ordinary limitations of everyday life. By immersing themselves in the mysteries of the craft and seeking to uncover the hidden truths beneath the surface, Freemasons embark on a transformative journey towards self-realization and enlightenment, guided by the timeless principles of truth, morality, and brotherly love.

CHAPTER 15

Final Revelations

As we delve further into the mysterious depths of Freemasonry, we find ourselves immersed in a world of symbolism and esoteric knowledge that transcends the boundaries of time and space. The final revelations of this ancient fraternity reveal a cosmic tapestry woven with intricate threads of wisdom, illuminated by the light of truth and reason.

The Freemason's symbolic journey parallels the journey of the individual seeking enlightenment and self-discovery. Each step along the path is laden with layers of meaning, inviting the initiate to contemplate the mysteries of existence and their place within the cosmic order. The symbols interwoven into the fabric of Freemasonry serve as signposts, guiding the wanderer towards a deeper understanding of themselves and the world around them.

At the heart of Freemasonry lies the concept of the Great Architect of the Universe, a transcendent force that imbues all creation with purpose and meaning. Through the rituals and ceremonies of the craft, initiates are encouraged to contemplate their relationship to this divine source and to align their actions with the principles of virtue and morality. The working tools of the craft take on a profound significance as symbols of inner transformation, reminding the Mason of the need to continually refine and perfect their character in pursuit of spiritual enlightenment.

The Temple of Solomon, both a historical edifice and a metaphorical representation of the human soul, serves as a focal point for Masonic teachings. Within its sacred precincts, initiates are encouraged to seek the hidden truths of existence and confront their own nature's shadow aspects. By facing their fears and flaws with courage and humility, the Mason can begin the inner alchemy process that transmutes base instincts into noble virtues.

The Temple's architecture symbolises the microcosm's construction within the macrocosm, reflecting the divine blueprint underlying all creation. The three pillars of Wisdom, Strength, and Beauty support the initiate's journey towards self-discovery and enlightenment. Through meditation, introspection, and contemplation, the Mason seeks to harmonize their inner trinity and align themselves with the higher principles of the universe.

The final revelations of Freemasonry do not mark the end of the journey but rather a new beginning, a threshold crossed into a realm of higher understanding and deeper insight. Through continued study, reflection, and practice, the Mason can unlock the secrets of the craft and integrate its teachings into every aspect of their life. The ultimate goal of the Freemasons is not merely personal enlightenment but the transformation of the world around them through acts of charity, compassion, and service.

May the final revelations of Freemasonry inspire us to continue our quest for truth, enlightenment, and self-improvement so that we may honour the legacy of this noble brotherhood and contribute to the evolution of humanity towards a brighter future filled with harmony, peace, and understanding.

The true essence of Freemasonry lies in the profound journey of self-discovery and spiritual enlightenment it offers its initiates. By peeling back the layers of symbolism and esoteric knowledge, the aspirant uncovers insights into the nature of existence and the interconnectedness of all things. The teachings of the craft are not merely intellectual exercises but transformative experiences that challenge the individual to confront their limitations and reach for higher realms of consciousness.

Central to the philosophy of Freemasonry is the idea of the individual as both a microcosm of the universe and a vessel for divine light. Through the practice of moral virtue, introspection, and service to others, the Freemason seeks to embody the ideals of wisdom, strength, and beauty in their daily life. The rituals and symbols of the craft serve as keys to unlocking the mysteries of the soul and elevating the initiate to a higher plane of existence.

The allegory of the Temple of Solomon, with its intricate architecture and sacred geometry, represents the inner sanctum of the self where the divine spark resides. By labouring to build this inner temple through self-discipline and self-improvement, the Mason aligns themselves with the universe's harmonies and attain a spiritual equilibrium state. The rough ashlar of the profane world is transformed into the smooth ashlar of the spiritual aspirant, reflecting the perfection and wholeness of the divine image.

In the final revelations of Freemasonry, the initiate realises that the secrets of the craft are not hidden in some distant place but are inscribed within the very fabric of their being. The journey of self-discovery is a lifelong pursuit, requiring dedication, humility, and a willingness to confront the shadows that lurk within. Through the teachings of Freemasonry, the individual can transmute their base instincts into noble virtues and bring light to the darkest corners of their soul.

May the final revelations of Freemasonry awaken a deeper understanding of ourselves, our place in the cosmos, and our interconnectedness with all beings. Let us walk the path of the Freemason with courage and conviction, striving always towards the light of truth and the perfection of our own divine nature.

CHAPTER 16

The Unveiling of Esoteric Knowledge

In the intricate tapestry of Freemasonry lies a profound and enigmatic realm that beckons the seeker to journey beyond the surface and into the depths of esoteric knowledge. The essence of Freemasonry transcends the ordinary realm of human understanding, offering a gateway to hidden truths and timeless wisdom safeguarded through the ages.

Esoteric knowledge, the hidden teachings that dwell at the core of Freemasonry, serves as a guiding light for those willing to embark on a transformative quest for inner enlightenment. It is a sacred repository of universal truths illuminating the path of spiritual evolution and self-discovery.

The symbolic language of Freemasonry is a rich tapestry woven with ancient wisdom, allegorical stories, and profound insights that point towards the mysteries of the universe and the divine nature of humanity. Each symbol, each ritual, and each lesson within Freemasonry carries a deeper meaning that invites the initiate to explore beyond the surface and into the hidden layers of esoteric knowledge.

At the heart of esoteric knowledge lies the concept of gnosis - a direct, experiential understanding of divine truths that transcends intellectual comprehension. Through the rituals and teachings of Freemasonry, initiates are guided on a journey of self-realization and spiritual awakening, where they come to recognize their inner light and divine nature.

The unveiling of esoteric knowledge within Freemasonry requires a process of inner reflection, contemplation, and spiritual growth. It is a journey of self-discovery that challenges the initiate to delve into the depths of their own being, confront their fears, limitations, and ego-driven desires, and emerge transformed with a renewed sense of purpose and clarity.

As the seeker progresses along the path of esoteric knowledge, they come to understand that the teachings of Freemasonry are not meant to be understood solely on an intellectual level. Instead, they are intended to be experienced, embodied, and integrated into one's being, transforming the initiate from within and awakening a deeper connection to the universal truths that govern the cosmos.

The journey of unveiling esoteric knowledge within Freemasonry is a sacred and profound quest that leads the seeker towards the realization of their inner divinity and the interconnectedness of all beings. A discovery, illumination, and transformation journey empowers the initiate to live a more conscious, purposeful, and meaningful life.

As the initiate delves deeper into the mysteries of esoteric knowledge, they begin to recognize the interconnectedness of all things and the underlying unity that binds the fabric of existence together. They come to understand that the external world is. Still, it is a reflection of the internal landscape, and that true transformation begins within.

The esoteric teachings of Freemasonry also shed light on the nature of spiritual evolution and the cyclical patterns of growth and renewal that govern both the individual soul and the collective consciousness of humanity. Through the symbolism of initiation, death, and rebirth, the initiate learns to embrace change, release old patterns and beliefs, and step into a new phase of self-realization and spiritual unfoldment.

At the heart of esoteric knowledge is recognising the divine spark within every being. This inner light, this sacred essence, is a reflection of the cosmic source of all creation, and it serves as a reminder of our inherent connection to the divine and to each other.

The journey of unveiling esoteric knowledge within Freemasonry is a sacred pilgrimage of the soul, a transformative odyssey that leads the initiate towards a deeper understanding of themselves, the universe, and the eternal mysteries that lie beyond the confines of time and space. It is a journey of self-discovery, self-transcendence, and self-realization that empowers the seeker to embody the highest ideals of Freemasonry and shine their light brightly in a world that needs illumination and love.

In the chapters that follow, we will continue to explore the depths of esoteric knowledge within Freemasonry, delving deeper into the mysteries of the cosmos, the nature of reality, and the profound implications of these teachings on our personal growth, our spiritual evolution, and our collective journey towards enlightenment.

CHAPTER 17

The Illumination of Truth

As we delve further into the labyrinthine depths of Freemasonry, we are met with a profound tapestry of symbolism, ritual, and teachings that beckons us to a higher understanding of truth. This truth, veiled in allegory and cloaked in mystery, is the cornerstone of our Masonic journey. This journey transcends the boundaries of time and space to illuminate the very essence of our existence.

Within the hallowed halls of the Masonic Lodge, we are reminded of the ancient quest for truth that has inspired seekers of wisdom throughout the ages. From the mystical traditions of antiquity to the esoteric teachings of alchemy and mysticism, the pursuit of truth has been a central theme in the perennial philosophy that underpins Freemasonry.

At the heart of Masonic symbolism lies the enigmatic figure of the "lost word" - a symbol of the ultimate truth that has been obscured from human understanding yet yearns to be revealed. Through the rituals of the craft, we are invited to contemplate the significance of this potent symbol and to meditate on the more profound implications of its hidden meaning.

Pursuing truth within Freemasonry is not a solitary endeavour but a collective journey of discovery and enlightenment. As we gather in brotherly unity within the lodge, we are reminded of the power of community and mutual support in our quest for truth. Through the bonds of friendship and fellowship, we are uplifted and inspired to continue our ascent towards the light of knowledge and understanding.

The illumination of truth in Freemasonry is not a static concept but a dynamic process of growth and evolution. Like the alchemical transformation of base metal into gold, our journey towards truth involves a profound inner alchemy that purifies our souls and awakens us to higher realities beyond the material realm.

As we progress through the degrees of Freemasonry, we are initiated into ever-deeper levels of understanding and insight, unveiling new layers of truth that challenge us to expand our consciousness and transcend our limitations. Through the craft's symbolic rituals and allegorical teachings, we are guided towards a profound realization of our divine nature and the interconnectedness of all life.

In the sacred space of the lodge, we are reminded of the eternal truths that lie at the core of our being - truths that transcend the temporal illusions of the material world and reveal the infinite realities that govern the universe. Through contemplation, meditation, and introspection, we recognise our inner light and our intrinsic connection to the divine source of all creation.

May the illumination of truth in Freemasonry continue to inspire us on our journey towards enlightenment and self-realization. May we, as custodians of the Masonic tradition, uphold the ancient principles of truth, wisdom, and virtue and serve as beacons of light in a world that dire needs guidance and inspiration. May the pursuit of truth within Freemasonry lead us to a deeper understanding of ourselves, our purpose, and our place in the vast tapestry of existence.

The journey towards truth in Freemasonry is a profound exploration of the mysteries of existence. This quest transcends the boundaries of the material world and delves into the realms of the divine. As we navigate the intricate web of symbolism and ritual that characterizes the Masonic tradition, we are exposed to profound truths that challenge our preconceptions and expand our understanding of the nature of reality.

Through the craft's allegorical teachings and symbolic imagery, we are invited to contemplate the deeper meanings beneath our everyday experiences. From the tools of the operative mason to the symbols of the speculative Mason, each aspect of the Masonic tradition serves as a gateway to a deeper understanding of the spiritual truths that underpin our existence.

Pursuing truth within Freemasonry is a transformative journey that requires dedication, introspection, and a willingness to embrace the unknown. As we progress through the degrees of the craft, we are initiated into new levels of awareness and insight, gaining a deeper appreciation for the interconnectedness of all existence and our place within the grand cosmic tapestry.

At the heart of the Masonic quest for truth lies the eternal search for the "lost word" - a symbol of the ultimate truth that lies at the core of our being and yet eludes our grasp. Our contemplation of this enigmatic symbol reminds us of the inherent mystery of existence and the eternal quest for enlightenment that drives us ever forward on our spiritual journey.

In the sacred space of the lodge, surrounded by our brethren and guided by the timeless teachings of the craft, we are reminded of the importance of seeking truth in all aspects of our lives. As we strive to embody the noble virtues of Freemasonry - truth, integrity, and honour - we are reminded of our profound responsibility as custodians of the ancient wisdom entrusted to us.

May the pursuit of truth within Freemasonry continue to inspire us to seek deeper meanings beneath the surface of our everyday experiences. May we be guided by the light of knowledge and understanding as we navigate the intricate terrain of Masonic symbolism and ritual. May we, as seekers of truth and wisdom, embody the noble principles of the craft in all we do, shining as beacons of light in a world that constantly needs enlightenment and inspiration.

CHAPTER 18

The Legacy Continues

As we delve into the rich history and profound teachings of Freemasonry, it becomes increasingly evident that the legacy of this venerable institution continues to endure through the passage of time. Rooted in ancient traditions and guided by timeless principles, Freemasonry has left an indelible mark on the world, shaping the lives of countless individuals and influencing the course of history.

The essence of this legacy lies in the unwavering commitment to uphold the values of brotherhood, integrity, and moral virtue. Freemasonry serves as a beacon of light in a world often shrouded in darkness, offering guidance and inspiration to those who seek truth and enlightenment. Freemasonry provides a pathway for personal growth and spiritual development through its rituals, symbols, and teachings, encouraging individuals to strive towards a higher plane of consciousness and understanding.

Freemasonry's origins can be traced back to the medieval stonemasons and guilds of Europe, who played a vital role in constructing the grand cathedrals and castles that still testify to their craftsmanship. These operative Masons, skilled in the art of building, operated under the strictest guidelines and traditions, passing down their knowledge from one generation to the next. Over time, as the demand for their services decreased, these craftsmen began to accept non-operatives into their ranks, forming the basis of speculative Freemasonry.

Freemasonry's rituals, symbols, and allegories are steeped in symbolism and mysticism, inviting initiates to contemplate deeper truths and uncover hidden meanings within themselves. The classic tools of the stonemason – the square, compasses, and plumb rule – are used metaphorically to teach moral lessons and guide individuals on the path to self-improvement. Through the initiation ceremonies and degree work, Freemasons are taken on a symbolic journey of self-discovery, where they are encouraged to reflect on their actions, thoughts, and beliefs.

The legacy of Freemasonry is also closely tied to the values of charity and service. Freemasons are encouraged to support their communities through philanthropy and volunteerism, embodying the spirit of selflessness and compassion. The Masonic principles of equality and tolerance foster a sense of unity and solidarity among members, transcending boundaries of race, religion, and social status.

As the custodians of this sacred tradition, Freemasons are responsible for ensuring that the legacy continues to thrive and evolve in the modern world. By upholding the principles of charity, tolerance, and mutual respect, Freemasonry remains a force for good in society, fostering unity and harmony among its members and the community.

The legacy of Freemasonry is a tapestry woven with threads of wisdom, compassion, and enlightenment. Its teachings, rituals, and symbols form a sacred language that speaks to the depths of the human soul, inviting initiates to explore the mysteries of existence and the nature of reality. Within the hallowed halls of the Masonic Lodge, seekers of truth and wisdom gather to contemplate the meaning of life, the purpose of our existence, and the interconnectedness of all things.

Freemasonry's legacy is one of profound significance, reaching back through the annals of time to the very origins of human civilization. The ancient wisdom preserved within its teachings offers a roadmap for personal transformation and spiritual awakening, guiding individuals on self-discovery and enlightenment. By adhering to the principles of brotherly love, relief, and truth, Freemasons honour the legacy of their forebears and uphold the sacred tradition passed down to them through generations.

In the spirit of continuity and tradition, we must carry forward the legacy of Freemasonry with reverence and dedication. By embodying the timeless principles of our Craft and embracing the values that have guided us for centuries, we ensure that the legacy of Freemasonry continues to shine brightly, illuminating the path towards a more enlightened and harmonious future.

May the legacy of Freemasonry endure for all time, serving as a testament to the enduring power of brotherhood, truth, and light.

May we, as Freemasons, continue to uphold and cherish this legacy, ensuring that it inspires and uplifts all who seek its wisdom.

CHAPTER 19

Exploring the Mysteries of Freemasonry

This chapter delves into the intriguing world of Freemasonry, a centuries-old fraternal organization steeped in tradition, symbolism, and esoteric knowledge. Freemasonry, often shrouded in mystery and misconceptions, offers its members a profound journey of self-discovery and enlightenment.

At the heart of Freemasonry are its teachings and rituals, carefully preserved and passed down through generations. Freemasonry's veiled symbols and allegories are rich with meaning and guide personal growth and moral development.

Through exploring Masonic teachings, initiates are encouraged to reflect on the deeper truths of existence and the interconnectedness of all things. The rituals of Freemasonry are designed to inspire contemplation and introspection, leading members on a path of self-improvement and the pursuit of Divine Truth.

As Masons progress through the degrees of Freemasonry, they uncover layers of symbolism and wisdom that challenge their perceptions and expand their understanding of the universe. The allegorical stories and moral lessons woven into Masonic teachings provide a framework for living a virtuous and meaningful life.

The mysteries of Freemasonry extend beyond the physical rituals and symbols, delving into the realms of philosophy, spirituality, and metaphysics. Through the study of Masonic philosophy, members are encouraged to seek knowledge, ask probing questions, and explore the depths of their own consciousness.

Freemasonry is a journey of self-discovery and enlightenment, a quest for truth and wisdom that transcends the boundaries of time and space. By exploring the mysteries of Freemasonry, one embarks on a sacred and transformative journey towards realising one's highest potential and uncovering the universal truths that govern one's existence.

The symbolic tools of the Masonic craft – the square, compass, plumb, and level – represent moral lessons and principles that guide Masons in their daily lives. The square teaches integrity and honesty, the compass teaches balance and harmony, the plumb teaches uprightness and self-awareness, and the level teaches equality and unity.

Freemasonry also emphasises the importance of brotherly love, relief, and truth. Brotherly love encourages Masons to treat all individuals with kindness and respect, recognizing the inherent worth and dignity of every human being. Relief prompts Masons to actively seek opportunities to help those in need, practising charity and compassion in their interactions with others.

Truth, as a fundamental tenet of Freemasonry, calls on members to seek truth in all aspects of their lives, embracing authenticity and honesty in their words and actions. By aligning their thoughts, words, and deeds with the guiding principles of Freemasonry, members strive to live virtuous and meaningful lives, contributing positively to their communities and the world at large.

The esoteric teachings of Freemasonry offer a profound exploration of the mysteries of existence, encouraging members to contemplate the nature of reality, the purpose of life, and the interconnectedness of all beings. Through introspection and self-examination, Masons uncover hidden truths and insights illuminating their path to personal growth and spiritual enlightenment.

Freemasonry serves as a sacred sanctuary for seekers of truth and wisdom, providing a platform for philosophical inquiry, spiritual contemplation, and moral reflection. By engaging with Freemasonry's timeless teachings and rituals, members embark on a transformative journey of self-discovery, inner alchemy, and realising their divine potential.

In the hallowed halls of Freemasonry, the flames of knowledge, wisdom, and enlightenment burn bright, guiding initiates on a sacred quest for self-realization and universal understanding. By embracing the mysteries of Freemasonry and delving into its depths, one unlocks the secrets of the universe and discovers the eternal truths that shape our existence.

The symbolism of Freemasonry extends into the very structure and organization of the fraternity itself. The hierarchical nature of Masonic lodges mirrors the progression of the individual seeker on their path towards enlightenment. Each degree represents a symbolic step in the initiate's journey, leading them towards a deeper understanding of themselves and their place in the world.

The sacred geometry present throughout Freemasonry reflects an ancient and mystical understanding of the universe. Symbols such as the circle, the triangle, and the pentagram convey profound truths about the nature of reality and the interconnectedness of all things. By contemplating these geometric shapes, Masons are encouraged to explore the harmonious order underlying the cosmos and recognize their own place within this grand design.

The rituals of Freemasonry are not merely symbolic performances but profound experiences that engage the senses, emotions, and intellect of the participants. Through the ceremonial initiation into each degree, candidates are guided through symbolic actions and teachings that awaken their inner consciousness and reveal hidden truths about themselves and the world around them.

The concept of light holds a central place in Masonic symbolism, representing knowledge, wisdom, and enlightenment. The symbolic journey from darkness to light, from ignorance to understanding, mirrors the spiritual evolution of the Masonic initiate as they progress through the degrees and uncover more profound mysteries of the craft. By seeking the light of knowledge and truth, Masons aspire to illuminate their minds and hearts, becoming beacons of wisdom and virtue in a world shrouded in darkness.

Freemasonry encourages its members to cultivate patience, tolerance, and humility in their interactions. By practising these virtues, Masons strive to embody the noble principles of the craft and to emulate the divine qualities that lie at the core of their being. Through acts of kindness, charity, and service, Masons seek to positively impact the world around them, uplifting those in need and spreading the light of Freemasonry to all corners of society.

The symbols of Freemasonry serve as keys to unlocking the deeper mysteries of existence and reveal profound insights into the nature of reality and the human experience. By meditating on these symbols and engaging with the teachings of the craft, Masons embark on a journey of self-discovery, spiritual transformation, and the realization of their highest potential. In the sacred brotherhood of Freemasonry, seekers of truth and wisdom find a nurturing and supportive community where they can explore the mysteries of existence and deepen their understanding of the universe and themselves.

The teachings of Freemasonry are not intended to provide easy answers or superficial truths but to challenge members to question their beliefs, confront their fears, and expand their consciousness. By engaging with the mysteries of Freemasonry, initiates embark on a journey of self-transformation, releasing old patterns of thought and behaviour to embrace new insights and perspectives.

The symbolism of the Masonic apron, worn by all members during lodge meetings, holds deep significance within Freemasonry. The white apron, symbolizing purity and virtue, reminds Masons of the moral responsibilities they have taken upon themselves. Through the symbolism of the apron, members are encouraged to strive for moral excellence, to uphold the values of the craft, and to lead lives of integrity and honour.

The Masonic ritual of the "cable tow" represents the bonds of duty and obligation that unite all Freemasons in their shared quest for knowledge and truth. The cable tow, a symbolic cord worn by candidates during initiation, signifies the interconnectedness of all members of the fraternity and the mutual support and guidance they offer one another on their Masonic journey.

The concept of secrecy within Freemasonry is often misunderstood, with some viewing it as a cloak of mystery and exclusivity. However, the true purpose of Masonic secrecy is not to withhold knowledge or truths from the world but to preserve the sanctity and integrity of the teachings within the fraternity. By safeguarding the sacred rituals, symbols, and doctrines of Freemasonry, members honour the ancient traditions of the craft and maintain the purity of its teachings for future generations.

Freemasonry also strongly emphasises the importance of self-improvement and personal growth. Through the study of Masonic teachings, engagement with the rituals and symbols of the craft, and participation in charitable activities, members are encouraged to cultivate virtues such as wisdom, compassion, and integrity. By striving for excellence in all aspects of their lives, Masons seeks to contribute positively to their communities and uphold the fraternity's noble principles.

The Masonic journey is a lifelong quest for knowledge, wisdom, and self-discovery. As Masons progress through the degrees of Freemasonry, they deepen their understanding of the craft's symbolic teachings and philosophical concepts. Each degree offers new insights and challenges, expanding the awareness and consciousness of the initiate as they progress toward enlightenment.

The fellowship and camaraderie found within Masonic lodges provide members with a supportive and nurturing environment where they can explore Freemasonry's mysteries and engage in meaningful discussions with like-minded seekers of truth. By coming together in brotherhood, Masons form deep and lasting bonds, sharing in each other's triumphs and challenges and offering mutual support and encouragement on their individual and collective journeys.

Freemasonry's rich heritage, ancient traditions, and timeless wisdom inspire seekers of truth and knowledge worldwide. By delving into the mysteries of Freemasonry, one embarks on a sacred and transformative journey of self-discovery, spiritual enlightenment, and the realization of one's divine potential. Through the exploration of the symbolic teachings and rituals of the craft, initiates uncover hidden truths, expand their awareness, and connect with the universal principles that govern the cosmos.

In the sacred brotherhood of Freemasonry, seekers of truth and wisdom find a path of light, love, and enlightenment, guiding them toward a deeper understanding of themselves, their place in the world, and the interconnectedness of all beings. By embracing the mysteries of Freemasonry and engaging with its profound teachings, members embark on a sacred quest for self-realization, inner alchemy, and uncovering the timeless truths that govern our existence.

As the flames of knowledge, wisdom, and enlightenment burn bright within the hallowed halls of Freemasonry, initiates are called to awaken their inner light, illuminate the darkness within, and embody the noble principles of the craft in their lives. By walking the path of Freemasonry with an open heart and mind, seekers of truth and wisdom can transcend the limitations of the material world, connect with the universal consciousness, and shine as beacons of divine light in a world needing guidance and inspiration.

The mysteries of Freemasonry are as vast and profound as the cosmos, offering initiates a sacred and transformative journey of self-discovery, spiritual awakening, and enlightenment. By engaging with the craft's symbolic teachings, rituals, and traditions, Masons uncover hidden truths, deepen their understanding of the universe, and connect with the eternal wisdom that flows through all things. In the mystical tapestry of Freemasonry, seekers of truth and wisdom find a powerful and transformative path toward personal growth, spiritual evolution, and the realization of their highest potential.

In the boundless expanse of Freemasonry, the seeker is invited to explore the deepest mysteries of existence, contemplate the eternal truths underlying the universe, and unlock the hidden wisdom within. Through the timeless teachings and rituals of the craft, initiates embark on a sacred quest for self-realization, spiritual enlightenment, and the revelation of the divine spark that resides within their souls. Freemasonry beckons all seekers of truth and wisdom to join in its sacred journey, to unveil the mysteries of the cosmos, and to awaken to the infinite possibilities that lie beyond the veil of ignorance.

CHAPTER 20

Unveiling the Mysteries Beyond Further Explorations

As we journey deeper into the enigmatic world of Freemasonry, we find ourselves immersed in a sea of profound symbolism, ancient teachings, and esoteric wisdom that beckon us to explore even further. In this chapter, we delve into the hidden realms of Masonic mysticism, where the veil between the material and spiritual worlds grows thin, revealing glimpses of transcendent truths that have been guarded and passed down through generations of Masonic brethren.

The symbols adorn the Masonic lodges and rituals serve as potent reminders of the universal principles underpinning the fabric of existence. From the square and compass to the blazing star and the pillars of wisdom, each symbol carries layers of meaning that invite us to contemplate the more profound mysteries of life, the universe, and our innermost being.

At the heart of Freemasonry lies the concept of the divine architect, the grand designer of the cosmos whose presence is reflected in the intricate geometries of sacred architecture and the harmonious order of the universe. This divine blueprint serves as a template for the spiritual evolution of the individual Mason, guiding them on a path of self-discovery, moral rectitude, and spiritual enlightenment.

The rituals of Freemasonry, shrouded in mystery and rich in symbolism, are a profound initiatory journey that takes the candidate through a series of transformative experiences designed to purify the heart, enlighten the mind, and uplift the soul. Through the solemn obligations, symbolic gestures, and profound teachings of the degrees, the Mason is led on a path of spiritual ascension that culminates in a deeper understanding of their place in the cosmic order.

As we navigate through the labyrinthine corridors of Masonic philosophy, we encounter a tapestry of esoteric knowledge that speaks to the innermost recesses of the soul. From the teachings of the ancient mysteries to the wisdom of the hermetic tradition, the Mason is invited to explore the hidden depths of human consciousness and the eternal truths that lie beyond the physical world's limitations.

The journey of the Freemason is a sacred pilgrimage, a quest for enlightenment that transcends the boundaries of time and space. Through diligent study, contemplation, and practice, the Mason is empowered to unlock the hidden chambers of the mind, to expand their consciousness, and to integrate the profound teachings of the craft into their everyday life.

Entering the sanctum sanctorum of Masonic wisdom, we confront the enigmatic concept of gnosis, the direct experiential knowledge of the divine that transcends mere intellectual understanding. In the inner sanctum of the lodge, the seeker is initiated into a sacred communion with the ineffable source of all existence. This transcendent experience defies description and transforms the very core of their being.

The esoteric teachings of Freemasonry draw upon a vast tapestry of ancient wisdom traditions, weaving together strands of Egyptian mysticism, Hebraic Kabbalah, alchemical symbolism, and Christian mysticism to create a holistic framework for spiritual growth and evolution. Through the symbolic language of allegory and ritual, the Mason is initiated into a timeless tradition of mystical inquiry that seeks to unveil the hidden truths of the universe and awaken the divine spark within each soul.

Masonic philosophy is deeply rooted in the symbolism of the initiate's journey, a profound metaphor for the soul's progression from ignorance to enlightenment. This journey is structured through three degrees of initiation, each representing a significant stage in the candidate's spiritual and personal development.

1. **Entered Apprentice**: This is the first degree of initiation, symbolizing the journey's beginning. The Entered Apprentice is introduced to the basic principles of Freemasonry and begins to learn the importance of moral and ethical behaviour. This stage emphasizes self-awareness and the recognition of one's ignorance, serving as the foundation for further growth. The candidate

undergoes symbolic rituals illustrating the initial steps from darkness (ignorance) into light (knowledge).
2. **Fellow Craft**: The second degree, Fellow Craft, represents the stage of further education and intellectual development. At this level, the candidate delves deeper into studying the liberal arts and sciences, promoting a broader understanding of the world and one's place. This stage signifies the ongoing journey towards wisdom, highlighting the importance of labour, skill, and the pursuit of knowledge.
3. **Master Mason**: The third and final degree, Master Mason, signifies the completion of the initial stages of enlightenment and the attainment of a higher level of understanding. This degree represents maturity, mastery, and the full realization of Masonic teachings. The rituals and symbols in this stage often focus on themes of immortality, moral fortitude, and the soul's ultimate destiny.

Throughout these degrees, the initiate faces various trials and challenges designed to test their character, resilience, and commitment to Masonic values. These experiences are intended to be transformative, encouraging personal and spiritual growth. The journey from Entered Apprentice to Master Mason is not merely a sequence of ceremonial steps but a symbolic representation of the transformative path of spiritual evolution, mirroring the soul's ascent from darkness to light.

In the depths of the Masonic temple, amidst the incense-laden air and the flickering candlelight, the initiate is guided on a journey of self-discovery and inner transformation that leads them to the threshold of divine illumination. Through the purification of the heart, the enlightenment of the mind, and the liberation of the soul, the Mason is initiated into the sublime mysteries of the craft and entrusted with the sacred knowledge that has been guarded and preserved through the ages.

As we peer beyond the veil of secrecy and symbolism that enshrouds Freemasonry, we catch glimpses of a profound spiritual tradition that speaks to the eternal quest for truth, beauty, and goodness. In the sacred precincts of the lodge, amidst the solemn rituals and mystical teachings, we discover a living tradition of esoteric wisdom that offers a transformative path to those who seek to unlock the hidden mysteries of existence and unite with the divine essence that animates all creation.

In the hallowed halls of Masonry, the seeker is initiated into a timeless brotherhood of truth-seekers and light-bearers who labour together in the great work of spiritual evolution and moral perfection. Through the bonds of fellowship and the shared pursuit of higher knowledge, the Mason is invited to partake in a sacred communion with the divine source of all creation and to embody the noble virtues of wisdom, strength, and beauty in their daily lives.

The path of the Freemason is a journey of self-discovery, spiritual growth, and moral rectitude that challenges the initiate to transcend the limitations of the material world and awaken to the eternal truths that lie at the heart of existence. Through the initiates rituals, symbolic teachings, and communal fellowship of the lodge, the Mason is guided on a transformative path that leads to a deeper understanding of themselves, the universe, and the divine source of all creation.

As we conclude this chapter of our exploration into the depths of Freemasonry, we are reminded of the eternal quest for truth and enlightenment that lies at the heart of the craft. Through the lodge's sacred rituals, profound teachings, and transformative experiences, the Mason is initiated into a timeless tradition of esoteric wisdom that beckons them to transcend the limitations of the material world and unite with the divine source of all existence. In the luminous rays of Masonic light, we glimpse the eternal truths illuminating the seeker's path and inspire us to continue our quest for spiritual growth, moral rectitude, and mystical communion with the ineffable mysteries of the cosmos.

CHAPTER 21

Origins of Freemasonry in Ancient Mystery Schools

In ancient times, long before the formal establishment of Freemasonry as we know it today, the roots of this secretive and symbolic tradition can be traced back to the ancient mystery schools. These mystery schools were esoteric institutions in various ancient civilizations, including Egypt, Greece, Rome, and Mesopotamia.

The mystery schools served as learning and spiritual development centres, where initiates were taught secret knowledge and wisdom inaccessible to the general public. These teachings encompassed various subjects, including philosophy, mathematics, astronomy, alchemy, and metaphysics.

Initiation into the mystery schools was a profound and transformative experience, where individuals underwent rituals, ceremonies, and teachings designed to impart hidden truths and spiritual insights. Through these experiences, initiates were believed to achieve a deeper understanding of themselves, the universe, and the divine, leading to personal growth and enlightenment.

The symbolism and allegories used in the mystery schools were rich and complex, often drawing upon mythological, astrological, and religious traditions to convey deeper meanings and truths. These symbols were believed to be the keys to unlocking hidden knowledge and spiritual enlightenment, guiding initiates on their self-discovery and inner transformation journey.

The foundations of Freemasonry were laid within this rich tapestry of ancient mystery traditions. The principles of secrecy, ritual, symbolism, and spiritual enlightenment that characterize Freemasonry today can be seen as a continuation of the ancient traditions practised in the mystery schools.

As Freemasonry evolved and developed over the centuries, it would draw upon these ancient roots to shape its unique identity and philosophy. The influence of the mystery schools can still be felt in the symbolic language, rituals, and teachings of Freemasonry, reminding us of the profound and timeless wisdom passed down through the ages.

The ancient mystery schools were not just about intellectual learning; they focused on transforming the initiate physically, emotionally, mentally, and spiritually. The initiates were taken through symbolic rituals representing various aspects of their journey towards enlightenment and self-realization.

These rituals often used sacred symbols, tools, and architectural elements with deeper meanings and spiritual significance. For example, using the square and compass in Freemasonry represents the importance of morality and self-discipline in leading a balanced and virtuous life.

The ancient mystery schools also incorporated teachings on the divine nature of the universe, the interconnectedness of all things, and the soul's journey towards reunion with the divine source. Initiates were encouraged to contemplate the mysteries of existence, the nature of reality, and their place within the cosmic order.

Through their studies and experiences in the mystery schools, initiates were challenged to expand their consciousness, transcend their egoic limitations, and connect with the higher aspects of their being. This inner transformation was seen as essential for achieving true wisdom, inner peace, and spiritual liberation.

In this way, the legacy of the ancient mystery schools continues to live on in the traditions of Freemasonry, offering seekers of truth and wisdom a path toward self-discovery, personal growth, and spiritual enlightenment. These ancient traditions' timeless principles and teachings remind us of the eternal quest for knowledge, understanding, and connection with the divine that has inspired seekers throughout the ages.

CHAPTER 22

Evolution of Freemasonry Among Medieval Stonemasons

In addition to their role as builders of magnificent architectural wonders, medieval stonemasons were also keepers of ancient wisdom and custodians of esoteric knowledge. Drawing upon traditions from antiquity, these craftsmen infused their work with symbols and teachings that transcended the mere physical act of construction. Each stone laid and arch raised held a structural purpose and a spiritual significance, representing a connection to the divine and the mysteries of the universe.

Central to the practices of these stonemasons were rituals and ceremonies that mirrored the cycles of nature and the journey of the soul. Through initiation rites and symbolic gestures, they welcomed new members into their ranks and imparted teachings on morality, virtue, and the interconnectedness of all living beings. With its sacred geometry and carefully arranged tools, the lodge itself served as a microcosm of the cosmic order, a reflection of the harmony and balance sought by those who walked the path of the craft.

As the stonemasons travelled from one construction site to another, they carried the tools of their trade and a repository of hidden knowledge passed down through generations. In their interactions with fellow artisans, they shared technical skills and deeper insights into the nature of reality and the quest for enlightenment. Over time, these teachings became enshrined in the rituals and symbols of Freemasonry, transforming the craft from a purely operative trade into a spiritual, philosophical tradition that sought to illuminate the minds and hearts of its initiates.

The transition from operative to speculative Freemasonry marked a pivotal moment in the evolution of the craft, as the fraternity expanded its membership to include men from diverse backgrounds and walks of life. No longer limited to stonecutters and builders, Freemasonry became a beacon for seekers of truth, wisdom, and spiritual growth. Its teachings on brotherly love, moral virtue, and personal development resonated with those who sought a deeper understanding of themselves and their place in the world.

Today, the legacy of the medieval stonemasons continues to inspire Freemasons worldwide as they gather in lodges to contemplate the timeless truths embedded in their rituals and symbols. Through study, reflection, and service to others, Freemasons seek to carry on the tradition of the craft, honouring the legacy of those who came before them and striving to build a more harmonious and enlightened society for future generations.

CHAPTER 23

Symbolism and Allegories in Freemasonry

In Freemasonry, symbolism is not merely a superficial layer of decoration but rather a profound language that speaks directly to the heart and soul of its members. Each symbol, each allegory, and each ritual carries layers of meaning and wisdom that are meant to be contemplated and internalized over a lifetime of Masonic journey.

The square and compasses, for instance, are not just tools of the trade but representations of the very essence of Freemasonry itself. The square, with its four equal sides, reminds us to walk with honesty and integrity in all our dealings to be fair and just in our interactions. It symbolizes the importance of upholding moral principles and standing firm in the face of temptation and adversity. The square's four sides also represent Freemasonry's four cardinal virtues - temperance, fortitude, prudence, and justice - the foundation upon which a Mason builds his moral character.

On the other hand, the compasses, with their ability to draw a circle and define boundaries, teach us the importance of self-restraint and self-discipline. They remind us to keep our desires, passions, and ambitions in check to not be led astray from the path of virtue and righteousness. The compasses symbolize the balanced pursuit of knowledge, wisdom, and understanding in our quest for personal and spiritual growth. The compasses remind us of the importance of maintaining balance in all aspects of our lives, ensuring we do not deviate from moral rectitude.

The volume of sacred law, whether the Bible, the Quran, the Torah, or any other religious text, serves as a cornerstone of moral guidance for Freemasons. It represents the eternal truths and timeless wisdom that transcend cultural and religious differences, uniting all Masons in their commitment to upholding ethical values and striving for personal improvement. The teachings and lessons within the volume of sacred law inspire Freemasons to lead lives of virtue, compassion, and service to others, embodying the principles of brotherly love, relief, and truth.

The allegorical stories woven into Masonic rituals are not just historical tales but powerful narratives that speak to universal themes of human nature and the quest for enlightenment. The building of King Solomon's temple, with its intricate design and skilled craftsmanship, serves as a metaphor for the Masonic journey– a lifelong endeavour of self-discovery, self-improvement, and the pursuit of inner light and truth. The temple symbolizes the inner sanctum of the Masonic initiate, where the individual seeks to purify his heart and mind, cultivate his intellect and spirit, and build a spiritual dwelling place fit for the indwelling of the Divine.

Likewise, the story of Hiram Abiff, the master builder who faced betrayal and death but remained faithful to his sacred duty, teaches Freemasons the virtues of fidelity, loyalty, and courage in the face of adversity. It serves as a reminder that true character is tested in times of trial and tribulation and that it is through perseverance and steadfastness that we can overcome the challenges that life presents us. The story of Hiram Abiff also symbolizes the journey of the soul through the trials and tribulations of earthly existence, with death representing not the end but a transformation into a higher state of being.

In essence, symbolism and allegory are not just decorative elements of Freemasonry but also essential components of its teachings and philosophy. They are the keys that unlock the hidden truths and deeper meanings of Masonic symbolism, guiding members on their journey towards self-discovery, self-improvement, and the realization of their highest potential as moral and upright individuals serving their communities and humanity. Through the contemplation and understanding of Masonic symbolism, Freemasons seek to embody the ideals of brotherhood, charity, and enlightenment, striving to make the world a better place through their words and actions.

CHAPTER 24

Spread of Freemasonry Across Europe

Freemasonry's spread across Europe in the early 18th century was a transformative phenomenon that transcended borders and social barriers, shaping the cultural and intellectual landscape of the continent. The establishment of the first Grand Lodge in England in 1717 marked the beginning of the Masonic movement, setting the stage for its expansion across various European countries. One of the driving forces behind Freemasonry's spread was its appeal to individuals from diverse backgrounds who sought connection, mutual support, and the pursuit of moral and spiritual enlightenment. The fraternity's core values of brotherhood, charity, and the search for truth resonated with many disillusioned with society's rigid hierarchies and organized religion. The military campaigns of the British Empire played a significant role in disseminating Freemasonry to different parts of Europe. British soldiers and officers, who were often Masons themselves, introduced the principles and rituals of the fraternity to local populations in regions as far-reaching as France, Germany, and Italy. This military connection facilitated the spread of Freemasonry. It helped foster a sense of camaraderie and shared purpose among Masonic brethren across borders. The Enlightenment period, emphasising reason, tolerance, and intellectual freedom, provided fertile ground for the growth of Freemasonry in Europe. Many Enlightenment thinkers, including Voltaire, Montesquieu, and Mozart, were known Freemasons who found in the fraternity a forum for exchanging ideas, promoting enlightened values, and advocating for social progress. The Masonic lodges became hubs of intellectual discourse and cultural exchange, attracting artists, writers, scientists, and philosophers who saw Freemasonry as a platform for advancing knowledge and humanistic ideals. As Freemasonry flourished across Europe during the 18th and 19th centuries, it spawned a rich tapestry of local traditions, rituals, and practices in different countries. Each Masonic jurisdiction and Grand Lodge developed its distinctive identity, blending universal Masonic principles with unique cultural elements, symbols, and ceremonies. This diversity enriched the Masonic experience and underscored the fraternity's ability to adapt and evolve in response to local customs and sensibilities. Despite facing opposition and persecution from religious and political authorities in some European countries, Freemasonry persevered, steadfast in its commitment to fostering brotherhood, charity, and moral integrity. The Masonic lodges served as sanctuaries of camaraderie and mutual support, offering a haven for individuals seeking fellowship, personal growth, and realising noble ideals. Freemasonry's impact on European society extended beyond the confines of its lodges, influencing art, literature, and political thought. Masonic symbols and ideals found their way into the works of prominent European artists and writers, such as Goethe, Blake, and Whistler, who drew inspiration from the fraternity's teachings of morality, symbolism, and self-improvement. The principles of Freemasonry also resonated with political reformers and revolutionaries who saw a model of a just and enlightened society based on equality, liberty, and fraternity in the fraternity. The spread of Freemasonry in Europe was not without its challenges and controversies. The fraternity's secretive nature and exclusive membership criteria sparked suspicion and mistrust among some segments of society, leading to accusations of conspiracy and subversion. Religious authorities, particularly the Catholic Church, viewed Freemasonry with scepticism and condemned it as incompatible with Christian doctrine, leading to the establishment of anti-Masonic movements in countries such as Spain, Portugal, and Italy.

Despite these challenges, Freemasonry continued to thrive in Europe, adapting to changing social, political, and cultural landscapes while remaining true to its core values of unity, tolerance, and mutual aid. The fraternity's global network of lodges and Grand Lodges provided a conduit for cross-cultural exchange and collaboration, fostering friendships and bonds of brotherhood that transcended national boundaries and linguistic barriers. In conclusion, Freemasonry's journey across Europe was a testament to the enduring power of fraternity, enlightenment, and human solidarity. The fraternity's spread left an indelible mark on European culture and history and laid the foundation for a global movement dedicated to unity, benevolence, and the ongoing quest for truth.

CHAPTER 25

Freemasonry During the Enlightenment Period

Freemasonry underwent a profound transformation during the Enlightenment period, paralleling the intellectual and societal changes that characterized this age of reason. As the Enlightenment emphasized critical thinking, scientific inquiry, and a rejection of traditional authority, Freemasonry provided a unique platform for like-minded individuals to gather, discuss, and advocate for these values. The influence of Freemasonry extended beyond Western Europe, spreading to the American colonies and reaching as far as the Middle East. In the new world, figures such as George Washington and Benjamin Franklin were active Freemasons, embodying the fraternity's principles of equality, liberty, and fraternity. The ideals of Freemasonry, embedded in its rituals and teachings, resonated with the spirit of independence and democratic governance that shaped the American Revolution.

Furthermore, Freemasonry served as a catalyst for social change and philanthropy during the Enlightenment period. Lodges across Europe and America engaged in charitable activities, supported education, and promoted the welfare of their communities. The "brotherly love" concept espoused by Freemasonry extended to fellow Masons and all humanity, reinforcing the importance of compassion and mutual support in a rapidly changing world. In addition, the symbolism of Freemasonry deepened during the Enlightenment, with allegorical teachings representing deeper philosophical truths. The operative mason's tools—the square, compass, and trowel—were moral instruments for shaping one's character and conduct. The square symbolized morality, the compass represented boundaries and self-control, and the trowel signified spreading brotherly love and unity. The beehive symbolized industriousness and cooperation within the Masonic Brotherhood, echoing the importance of diligence and collective effort in achieving common goals. The mosaic pavement underscored the dual nature of human existence: light and darkness, good and evil, and the continuous struggle to strive towards higher ideals and moral conduct. The rituals and ceremonies of Freemasonry once shrouded in secrecy, became more accessible and standardized during the Enlightenment period. Grand Lodges emerged as a governing body, providing structure and cohesion to the fraternity while safeguarding its core principles. Freemasonry's commitment to moral and intellectual development resonated with the values of the Enlightenment, fostering a community of individuals dedicated to self-improvement, the pursuit of truth, and the cultivation of virtue. Freemasonry flourished during the Enlightenment as a bastion of reason, tolerance, and progress. Its influence on the intellectual, social, and political landscape of the time was substantial, shaping the emergence of democratic ideals and paving the way for a more enlightened society. The fraternity's ability to adapt to the changing times while upholding its foundational principles ensured its enduring relevance and impact in an ever-evolving world.

CHAPTER 26

The Grand Lodge of England and Formalization of Freemasonry

The Grand Lodge of England holds a special place in the history and development of Freemasonry. Established in London in 1717, the Grand Lodge marked a significant turning point for the craft, bringing together disparate lodges and creating a more cohesive and organized structure. Under the leadership of the first Grand Master, Anthony Sayer, the Grand Lodge of England set out to formalize the practices and rituals of Freemasonry. One of the critical initiatives of the Grand Lodge was the standardization of rituals, ensuring that the core teachings and symbolism of the craft remained consistent across lodges. This standardization helped foster a sense of unity and shared purpose among Freemasons, regardless of their geographical location. In addition to ritual standardization, the Grand Lodge of England played a crucial role in establishing a system of governance for Freemasonry. By creating bylaws and regulations, the Grand Lodge outlined the roles and responsibilities of lodge officers and procedures for admitting new members. This framework provided a foundation for orderly conduct within the fraternity and helped maintain the integrity of the craft. The influence of the Grand Lodge of England extended beyond its borders, as its principles and practices were adopted by Masonic bodies in other countries. This led to the formation of Grand Lodges around the world, each with its own unique history and traditions but united by a joint commitment to the principles of Freemasonry. The Grand Lodge of England's legacy continues to resonate in the modern Masonic landscape, serving as a model for governance and organization within the fraternity. Its establishment marked a pivotal moment in the evolution of Freemasonry, shaping its trajectory and guiding its growth into a worldwide brotherhood based on principles of brotherly love, relief, and truth.

Furthermore, the Grand Lodge of England's commitment to intellectual pursuits and moral teachings has also impacted the craft. Encouraging philosophical discussions and promoting ethical behaviour, the Grand Lodge helped instil a sense of personal growth and enlightenment among its members. This emphasis on education and self-improvement remains a core aspect of Freemasonry, as lodges continue to provide a space for intellectual exploration and moral development.

Additionally, the Grand Lodge of England's dedication to charity and community service has been a defining characteristic of the craft. Freemasons uphold the values of compassion and benevolence central to the fraternity by relieving those in need and engaging in philanthropic endeavours. The Grand Lodge's early emphasis on charity set a precedent for Freemasons worldwide to actively contribute to the betterment of society, embodying the principles of service and altruism that are fundamental to Freemasonry. In conclusion, Freemasonry's Grand Lodge of England is a beacon of tradition and innovation. Its legacy of ritual standardization, governance, intellectual pursuit, moral teachings, charity, and community service continues to shape the practices and values of the craft, inspiring Freemasons around the globe to uphold the principles of brotherly love, relief, and truth.

CHAPTER 23

Rituals and Degrees of Freemasonry

In Freemasonry, rituals and degrees serve as the cornerstone of the craft, embodying profound teachings and timeless wisdom that guide members on a symbolic journey of self-discovery and moral enlightenment. These sacred ceremonies are steeped in tradition and symbolism, drawing upon the rich legacy of ancient mystery traditions and philosophical principles to impart valuable lessons and inspire personal growth. The structure of Freemasonry degrees, representing the three symbolic levels of Entered Apprentice, Fellowcraft, and Master Mason, reflects a systematic progression through stages of initiation and instruction. Each degree is a carefully crafted experience designed to lead the candidate through allegorical lessons, imparting moral virtues and encouraging introspection on the deeper truths of existence. Initiation rituals in Freemasonry hold a special significance, marking the candidate's transition from a profane state of ignorance and darkness to one of enlightenment and spiritual insight. Through symbolic rites of passage, individuals are challenged to confront their innermost fears, confront their shortcomings, and strive for personal development in alignment with the principles of the craft.

Central to Freemasonry's teachings are the myriad symbols and allegories that permeate its rituals, conveying profound truths and esoteric knowledge through a visual language of metaphor and analogy. From the tracing board to the working tools of the craft, each symbol carries layers of meaning that encourage contemplation and introspection, inviting members to delve deeper into the mysteries of existence and the nature of reality. The allegorical narratives embedded within Freemasonry rituals offer a roadmap for members to navigate the complexities of life, guiding them towards a path of moral rectitude, personal integrity, and spiritual enlightenment. By embodying the virtues of charity, tolerance, and brotherly love advocated by the craft, Freemasons cultivate a sense of duty towards self-improvement and service to humanity, uniting them in a common quest for truth and enlightenment. In essence, the rituals and degrees of

Freemasonry represent more than ceremonial practices—they are transformative experiences that shape the hearts and minds of members, instilling within them a deep sense of purpose, fellowship, and moral responsibility. Through their participation in these sacred rites, Freemason's forge bonds of brotherhood, cultivate a reverence for knowledge and virtue, and uphold the timeless values that have guided their craft through the ages.

CHAPTER 24

Freemasonry's Commitment to Charity and Community Service

Freemasonry's tradition of charitable work is deeply rooted in its historical origins and enduring principles of brotherhood, relief, and truth. From its earliest days in the 17th century, Freemasonry has been dedicated to supporting its members in times of need and extending its charitable endeavours to benefit the wider community. The concept of charity in Freemasonry goes beyond mere financial assistance to embody a holistic approach to helping those in need. Masonic lodges strive to provide monetary aid, practical support, and emotional guidance to their members facing hardships. By creating a sense of solidarity and mutual care, Freemasonry fosters an environment of compassion and understanding that transcends social boundaries. One of the distinctive features of Masonic charity is its emphasis on discretion and anonymity. Freemasons believe in the importance of humility and selfless service, choosing to carry out their charitable deeds without seeking recognition or praise. This commitment to quiet philanthropy underscores the fraternity's belief in the intrinsic value of helping others without expecting anything in return.

Furthermore, Freemasonry's charitable efforts are deeply interconnected with its commitment to personal growth and moral development. By engaging in acts of charity and service, Freemasons practice the values of kindness, compassion, and generosity, cultivating a sense of responsibility toward improving the well-being of individuals and society. On a broader scale, Masonic charities engage in long-term philanthropic initiatives that address systemic issues and create sustainable change. Whether through funding educational programs, supporting medical research, or assisting marginalized communities, Freemasons work tirelessly to make a positive impact and uphold their commitment to making a difference. Internationally, Freemasonry is vital in promoting humanitarian efforts and fostering international cooperation. By collaborating with global organizations and participating in relief efforts in areas affected by natural disasters and conflict, Masonic charities demonstrate their dedication to building bridges across cultures and advocating for peace and understanding on a global scale. Freemasonry's tradition of charity is a testament to its enduring values of solidarity, compassion, and service. By embodying these principles in their charitable work, Freemasons continue to inspire positive change, foster community, and uphold the timeless ideals of brotherhood and benevolence that define the fraternity.

CHAPTER 25

Freemasonry as a Path to Self-Improvement

Freemasonry, with its origins shrouded in the mists of time, stands as a beacon of light in the search for truth, wisdom, and self-discovery. The ancient roots of Freemasonry trace back to the guilds of stonemasons who built the magnificent cathedrals and castles of the medieval era, where craft secrets were passed down through the generations alongside moral teachings and spiritual insights. As the craft of stonemasonry waned, the symbolic tools and rituals of the trade were transformed into a philosophical and ethical system that transcended the building trade, evolving into the speculative Freemasonry we know today. Central to Freemasonry's teachings is the "journey of the soul," a symbolic pilgrimage towards inner enlightenment and self-improvement. Through a series of allegorical dramas and symbolic teachings, Freemasonry guides its members on a transformative path of self-discovery, encouraging them to reflect on their beliefs, values, and actions in the quest for personal growth and moral development. The symbolic tools of the mason— the square, compasses, and other working tools— serve as metaphors for the virtues of morality, integrity, and personal responsibility that underpin the Masonic teachings. Moreover, Freemasonry is a repository of ancient wisdom and esoteric traditions, drawing inspiration from diverse sources such as Hermeticism, Kabbalah, alchemy, and the teachings of the ancient mystery schools. By delving into these rich and varied philosophical traditions, Freemasons seek to unlock the hidden meaning behind the symbols and rituals of the Craft, uncovering more profound truths about the nature of reality, the mysteries of existence, and the human experience.

Furthermore, Freemasonry emphasizes the importance of intellectual inquiry and continual education as essential tools for personal growth and enlightenment. By studying the sacred texts, allegorical stories, and philosophical treatises that form the foundation of Masonic teachings, members engage in a lifelong pursuit of knowledge, seeking to expand their minds, challenge their preconceptions, and deepen their understanding of the world around them. "working in the quarries of the mind" enables Freemasons to sharpen their intellect, cultivate their critical thinking skills, and gain insight into the deeper meanings hidden within the layers of symbolism and metaphor that characterize Masonic rituals and teachings. Freemasons find a unique sanctuary for spiritual reflection, moral contemplation, and communal fellowship in the sacred precincts of the lodge. Through the shared experiences of the ritual ceremonies, the bonds of brotherhood, and the supportive network of fellow members, Freemasonry provides a supportive and nurturing environment for personal growth and self-improvement. Within the fraternity of the lodge, members find encouragement, guidance, and inspiration to embark on the challenging path of self-discovery, self-mastery, and self-transformation. In conclusion, Freemasonry is a timeless and enduring tradition that offers a profound and multifaceted framework for personal growth, moral development, and spiritual enlightenment. With its rich tapestry of symbolism, ritual, philosophy, and community, Freemasonry provides a path for individuals to explore the depths of their own souls, expand their minds, nurture their spirits, and strive toward the ideals of truth, virtue, and brotherly love. In the sacred precincts of the lodge, amidst the symbols and ceremonies of the Craft, Freemasons find a sanctuary for inner reflection, outer transformation, and the eternal quest for self-improvement and self-realization.

CHAPTER 26

The Enduring Principles of Freemasonry
Freemasonry is a venerable institution that has stood the test of time, drawing upon a rich tapestry of traditions and teachings passed down through generations of Masonic brethren. At its core, Freemasonry is founded on the timeless principles of brotherly love, relief, and truth, serving as guiding lights for members seeking to walk the path of enlightenment and self-improvement. Sisterly love is more than just a sentiment within Freemasonry; it is a profound commitment to fostering unity and understanding among individuals of diverse backgrounds and experiences. Through the bonds of fraternal friendship, Freemasons come together as one, transcending divisions of race, religion, and social status to form a unified brotherhood. This spirit of brotherly love creates a supportive and inclusive environment where all members are valued and respected, contributing to a sense of belonging and camaraderie cherished by Masons worldwide. Relief, a cornerstone of Masonic practice, embodies the ethos of charity and benevolence at Freemasonry's heart. Freemasons are dedicated to providing aid and support to those in need, whether within the Masonic family or the broader community. Through charitable works, relief efforts, and philanthropic initiatives, Freemasons extend a helping hand to alleviate suffering, promote well-being, and make a positive impact on the lives of others. This commitment to relief underscores Freemasonry's compassionate and altruistic nature, serving as a beacon of hope and assistance for individuals facing adversity or hardship. Truth, the third pillar of Freemasonry, symbolizes the pursuit of knowledge, wisdom, and moral integrity in the quest for personal and Masonic enlightenment. Freemasons are encouraged to seek truth in all aspects of their lives, embracing honesty, integrity, and ethical conduct as guiding principles. By upholding the ideals of truth and integrity, Freemasons strive to lead virtuous lives grounded in moral values and principles that inspire them to make meaningful contributions to society and uphold the highest standards of ethical behaviour. Through the enduring principles of brotherly love, relief, and

truth, Freemasonry continues to inspire, educate, and empower its members to lead lives of purpose, service, and integrity. As Masons strive to embody these foundational principles in their daily lives, they honour the fraternity's traditions and contribute to a legacy of brotherhood, compassion, and enlightenment that transcends time and geography.

CHAPTER 27

Epilogue: The Journey Continues

Remember, once you are a mason, you will always be a mason, even if you leave.
As we come to the end of this exploration into the world of Freemasonry, it is crucial to delve deeper into the profound and enduring impact that this ancient fraternity has had on society and the lives of its members. Freemasonry's history has continued to captivate and inspire individuals seeking more profound meaning, brotherhood, and moral enlightenment. The core principles of Freemasonry - brotherly love, relief, and truth - serve as pillars that uphold the essence of being a Mason. These values are not merely words to be spoken but virtues to be lived and embodied in every aspect of Mason's life. Through the practice of these principles, Masons strive to cultivate a sense of unity, compassion, and integrity in their interactions with others, fostering a community built on mutual respect and understanding. The symbolism inherent within Freemasonry's rituals and teachings adds depth to the Masonic experience. Each symbol, from the square and compass to the operative mason's tools, carries profound significance and offers valuable lessons for personal growth and self-reflection. These symbols serve as metaphors for the inner journey that each Mason undertakes, guiding them through stages of initiation, contemplation, and enlightenment. At the heart of Freemasonry lies a commitment to self-improvement and moral development. Freemasonry's initiation rituals and degrees are designed to challenge members to confront their shortcomings, reflect on their values and beliefs, and strive for a higher standard of conduct in their personal and professional lives. By embracing these challenges and dedicating themselves to the pursuit of knowledge and virtue, Masons can transform themselves into better individuals and contribute positively to the world around them. Beyond the individual journey of self-discovery, Freemasonry also emphasizes the importance of service and philanthropy. Masonic organizations are renowned for their charitable work, supporting various causes

and initiatives that benefit needy communities. Through acts of kindness, generosity, and compassion, Masons exemplify the principle of relief and demonstrate their commitment to positively impacting the world around them. As we look towards the future, the legacy of Freemasonry continues to shine brightly, offering a beacon of hope and inspiration to those who seek guidance, fellowship, and a deeper connection to the moral and spiritual truths that underpin our existence. The lessons learned within the lodge, the bonds of brotherhood forged in friendship, and the values instilled through Masonic teachings serve as a foundation upon which individuals can build a life of purpose, meaning, and service to others. The journey of a Mason is one of continual growth, enlightenment, and service. It is a path that invites us to delve deeper into the mysteries of the universe, to question our assumptions, and to strive for a more harmonious and just society. As we walk this path together, remember Freemasonry's timeless wisdom and profound impact on our lives and the world around us. May we continue to embody the principles of brotherly love, relief, and truth in all that we do, and may we uphold the sacred traditions of Freemasonry with reverence and dedication, ensuring that its light continues to shine brightly for generations to come. The legacy of Freemasonry transcends the passage of time. It inspires individuals to seek enlightenment and uphold brotherhood, unity, and moral integrity. Freemasonry's teachings offer a roadmap for navigating the complexities of life, guiding members towards a deeper understanding of themselves and their place in the world. Through the bonds of fraternal friendship and the shared commitment to personal growth and service, Masons finds strength and resilience in facing life's challenges with grace and grit. Freemasonry's beauty is its ability to bridge gaps, transcend differences, and unite individuals from diverse backgrounds for a common purpose. Across continents and cultures, Masons come together in harmony, bound by their mutual respect for one another and their shared dedication to upholding the principles that define Freemasonry. In a world often characterized by division and discord, Freemasonry stands as a beacon of unity and cooperation, demonstrating the power of brotherhood to overcome barriers and build bridges of understanding and compassion. As Masons continue their journey of self-discovery and moral enlightenment, they carry with them the wisdom and teachings of Freemasonry, shaping their lives and interactions with others in profound ways. Freemasonry's spirit lives on in its members' hearts and minds, guiding them towards a higher standard of conduct and inspiring them to positively impact their communities and the world. Through their actions and commitment to service, Masons embody the ideals of brotherly love, relief, and truth, serving as beacons of light in a world often overshadowed by darkness and uncertainty. In closing, let us remember that the journey of a Mason is one of continual growth, learning, and service. As we move forward, let us carry with us the lessons of Freemasonry, the bonds of brotherhood that unite us, and the enduring values that shape our lives. May we walk this path with humility, courage, and dedication, guided by the light of Freemasonry and the principles that define us as Masons. Together, let us strive to make a meaningful and lasting impact on the world, leaving a legacy of compassion, wisdom, and goodwill for future generations.

About the author

David Dowson has taken a compelling mystery from our history books and brought it to life in the 21st Century. David is risking everything by publishing this book.

He is a former British Intelligence Officer at GCHQ and a Professor of Chess Psychology. I have been playing chess for 40 years.

He has written several books on CHESS and over 43 various BOOKS Novels & KINDLE.

He is also a professionally trained Artist with a Black Belt in Tae Kwon Do.

He is an active freemason and plays classical music on the clarinet and keyboards.

IT computer expert specialising in chess computing programming,

He is a Master Freemason, Knights Templar and other degrees. Including the Illuminati and Opus Dei.

Printed in Great Britain
by Amazon

4ff66bf9-e7be-45f4-80b8-8020118be822R01